The junior church programme with a difference!

Three + One
The Law and the Prophets

Michael Forster

Kevin Mayhew

First published in 2002 by
KEVIN MAYHEW LTD
Buxhall, Stowmarket, Suffolk IP14 3BW
E-mail: info@kevinmayhewltd.com

9 8 7 6 5 4 3 2 1 0

ISBN 1 84003 889 6
Catalogue No 1500495

Cover design by Angela Selfe
Illustrated by Brent Clark
Edited by Katherine Laidler
Typesetting by Louise Selfe
Printed in Great Britain

Contents

Foreword

This series of books takes what might to many people seem to be a new approach to Junior Church teaching and all-age worship. In fact, though, it's a very old one – used, according to the Gospels, by Jesus himself.

First and foremost, Jesus valued people, cared about them, was concerned for their needs. He called people to become part of a community where they – many of them for the first time – were valued and enabled to feel that they were part of something worthwhile, that their lives had meaning and purpose. In the course of that, they learned a great deal and their commitment to Jesus and what he stood for grew until in many cases it was a life-commitment in more ways than one.

So the approach we take here is to focus on building relationships – including the children in something they may come to value, telling the faith story in engaging ways and letting the 'learning' be a spin-off benefit. I am convinced that that is a more effective way of working with children than focusing just on the imparting of knowledge.

People often complain that youth organisations do not seem 'interested in the Church'. The reality is that there is no *reason* for them to be interested: without faith commitment there is no other point in going to church when everything else it offers can be had more easily and more satisfyingly elsewhere. And that faith commitment will, I believe, be built more effectively, in their early years, by making them part of something they value *because it values them* rather than by trying to teach them things.

That brings me to the vital difference that sets this material apart. The sessions are arranged in sets of four: three 'Junior Church' sessions building into an all-age service on the fourth Sunday when the children's work will be celebrated and valued by the whole Church fellowship, and the adults will have the opportunity to learn both from and with the children.

I hope and pray that these resources will open minds of all ages to the wonder of God's love and the joy of sharing it, rather than merely fill them up with doctrines and ethical propositions.

All that will follow. The first thing – and the vital thing – is to *relate*.

Enjoy the book. Enjoy one another. Oh, and enjoy God, of course!

MICHAEL FORSTER

Introduction

(Please read this – I think you're going to like it!)

This series of books arose out of a particular need. We were finding the usual age-based 'classes' difficult to sustain in our context, and mixed-age groups seemed the only option – but the cry went up, 'You can't teach five- and ten-year-olds in the same class' (I'll have more to say about the 'teaching' idea later).

At the same time, we wanted to include the children much more in the actual planning of our monthly all-age worship which, until then, tended to be a bit of a one-man show that was done *for* rather than *with* them. But just when do you gather increasingly busy and pressurised children together to plan services?

This is what we decided to do. We would take an overall theme that could be presented in three weekly stories, and the learning process would consist of fun activities: story-telling, art and craft, drama, music, some of which could then become the basis for the all-age service. But what if some children could only come for two of the weeks? Would they be left out? Clearly, each week's story, while relating to the three-week theme, would need to be able to stand alone.

Wouldn't it make the all-age worship terribly long and overladen with material? Probably, if *all* the previous three-weeks' work were used – so the Junior Church would choose just one of the three stories as the focus for the service, but let the worship leader put it into context with the help of the pictures, models, etc., that the children had made. That would enable most of the art and craftwork to be on display in the church, providing a visual background to the storytelling. And storytelling really is the basis of communicating our faith. Ask any of our Jewish cousins! Or ask Jesus!

So this material was written, and some of it has been used, and the basic idea and format have been tried and tested. The result so far has been the releasing of some previously unrecognised creativity as children who had not been in the limelight before took the basic ideas and developed them in wonderfully imaginative ways. In the very first month of using this material, we discovered some real hidden treasure – and we did so in worship where we could properly celebrate and give thanks for it.

And that brings me to the most important thing we learned from this. Don't let the all-age worship become a talking shop! The discussion-type activities will quickly lose their appeal if that happens. We saw this coming in good time and proposed the setting up of a Worship and Mission Action Group (definitely *not* a committee) within the church to carry forward some of the ideas that come out of these sessions. Such a group must be a 'ginger group' rather than a management committee. They should not get bogged down in the minutiae of keeping new projects going, but simply research ideas and present possibilities to the relevant meetings (more than once if necessary!) to ensure that they are not simply lost in a sea of good intentions. If that were to happen – if the cards, etc., that the discussion groups produce were simply thrown away or filed and forgotten, we think it would not be long before the worship became stale: 'Oh, another of those silly discussions, again.' However, if the action group is set up, and enabled to work well, the all-age worship could become a real source of inspiration for the Church's mission – something through which the Holy Spirit might breathe renewal into the Church and the local community.

How to get the best from this book

The book is based on three 'units', each of which is a four-week cycle: three Junior Church sessions, and one all-age worship. Those Churches that currently have a monthly 'family service' will find it best to plan so that the 'fourth' Sunday in each unit falls on whatever Sunday of the month is appropriate for their system. (When there are five Sundays, that's not a problem – you'll appreciate the extra time to pull the threads together all the more firmly ready for the all-age service.)

Each session divides into a number of activities, and a worksheet is also provided either to do in the session or as a take-home resource. There will almost certainly be too much here for the single session of perhaps 45 minutes that most Junior Churches have – so *don't think you have to use it all.* (Nothing destroys a good learning environment like trying to cram too much in!) Choose what you think best fits your group in each particular case, and perhaps have other items standing by in case you run out. Much of course will depend on the number of children you have. A small Junior Church could work all together, concentrating on the story and just one or two activities, whereas a large one might start together for the storytelling and then break up into several multi-age groups, each focusing on a different activity – some children producing art and craft work, others doing drama, learning new songs, etc.

Similarly, you don't need necessarily to use all of sessions one to three. You may decide, in particular circumstances, to omit one session and spread the other two over the three weeks. The stories are written as stand-alone units, so you can do this quite easily. At the risk of labouring the point, the all-age worship in Week Four should be a celebration of whatever has been done – not a goal to be striven for and which becomes a blight on the sessions because the children are under pressure.

Most importantly of all, remember the central aims: the session should:

• be enjoyable for all concerned

• make all the children feel valued and cared about

• contribute to building relationships.

If you do these things, then the 'teaching' will happen, because children are great learners if the environment is right. They'll virtually teach themselves!

Let's have a look at each of the elements that comprise the sessions.

Thinking about it

This is vital – the advance preparation need not be unduly time-consuming or tedious, but it will transform the actual session. In fact, we found that the preparation required in using this material was much less onerous than preparing traditional lessons.

• A monthly meeting of key people would be a good idea, perhaps after Week Three, when you can pull together the all-age service and look ahead to the next four weeks.

- Consider which week's sub-theme will form the basis of the all-age worship. You may find it helpful to know this at the outset so that you will know which week's 'ticked' activity to prepare and which you can ignore.
- Then each week look through the relevant session thoroughly and give some thought to which would be the most appropriate and helpful elements to concentrate on, in your situation.
- Prepare any resources: art/craft materials, visual aids, legitimate photocopies, etc., that you need. Try to anticipate the kinds of questions the children might ask – or that you could helpfully ask them.

What's the point?

It's helpful to have a specific point in mind that we wish to convey. This does not mean we can't find other things in the text, but one point retained is better than five confused or forgotten – and more likely to engage the children's attention, too! They have the rest of their lives to explore the countless layers of meaning, so don't let's spoil it by cramming them too full of rich food!

Now for the session itself.

Doing it

Prayer

An opening prayer is offered. However, we should be careful about stereo-typing prayer too much as merely 'talking to God'. It might be worth thinking about encouraging children to think of prayer as consciously *being with* God – sometimes quietly, but also in the more active parts of life. So let God join in the activities, the fun, most of all in the growing *relationships* between staff, parents and children. In a different kind of way, the whole session is 'prayer' – and both kinds are important.

For this reason, the prayers are short and are all focused in such a way as to point the children to that greater reality: the unconditional love of God.

From the known to the unknown

Jesus understood well the first principle of teaching: begin with what people know, and only then introduce the new. His most effective teaching, according to the Gospel records, was in parables. Often, he simply didn't mention scripture at all.

That is not an argument against biblical teaching – rather it is a plea to make it more effective. Children are wonderful at making connections – much better than we adults with our 'disciplined' (trammelled?) minds. So we begin by appealing to what they know, and *then* tell them the biblical story. With little or no prompting, they often will then grasp joyfully and spontaneously for themselves what we so often labour painfully and inef-fectually to drill into them – and no one's more guilty of that than I am!

Tell the story

Story-telling is the basis of keeping the faith alive. Our Jewish forebears kept their children in the faith by telling and retelling vibrant stories, often around meal tables, campfires or in other informal settings, with plenty of song and laughter to help it along. So a child-friendly version of a Bible story is the mainstay of each week's material. It's a good idea to read it a few times in advance, so you are familiar and can half-tell, half-read it to the children with plenty of eye contact and other interaction. Or you can get them to tell it to each other by acting it out – see 'Drama', below. You may also find it useful to have some visual aids handy, or think of some questions you can ask, breaking off from the narrative whenever you choose to ask, 'How do you think God felt about that?' 'What d'you think happened then?' 'What would you have done about that?' etc. This will all help to maintain the children's interest – with a little imagination you can easily keep them enthralled!

Respond to the story

The children's response to the story now forms the basis of the rest of the session. It's important that they're encouraged to be spontaneous and really engage with the characters and the action. Here you will of course want to focus on the forms of response that are best suited to your situation, but the first one, 'Discussion', should never be missed out.

Discussion

Keep it lively, informal, chatty – and don't let any child feel silly or wrong, whatever they say or ask. The important thing is that they grow by being able to interact freely with the text. You may want to feed in some of their questions or reactions to the storytelling in the all-age worship. Most importantly, don't be anxious about this section – and don't let the discussion become either too long or too heavy! Just enjoy a bit of a chat with the children.

Song

Some songs are suggested. Either revisiting well-known ones or learning new ones can be fun, and perhaps sometimes the children can teach some of the new ones to the adults in the all-age worship. However, be careful not to let the Junior Church session degenerate into mere rehearsal. Let them have fun singing the songs, confident that even imperfectly sung they will still form acceptable worship. If some of the children have instruments, there's no reason why they couldn't be used at this time. All the songs recommended in these pages can be found in one or more of the following Kevin Mayhew publications (among others):

- *Kidsource*
- *The Source*
- *The Children's Hymn Book*
- *21st Century Folk Hymnal*

Art and craft

This will probably form quite a big part of the session: children of all ages and abilities can work together to produce models, drawings, paintings, etc. A few ideas are suggested, but they don't need to be limited. This was the area where we found children really showed their ingenuity and made immensely valuable contributions, producing and effecting ideas that would never have occurred to us!

Some of the art and craft work will feed into the all-age worship, and the items especially designed to do that are indicated with a tick. You may want to put less emphasis on this item if you're not planning on focusing on it in the service. What is important, in the 'ticked' activities, is that the children know *why* they are preparing these things – a few simple words of explanation will help them to relate it to the story they have heard and the point you were trying to make.

In terms of drawing and painting, the options are limited only by size of the group and the children's imaginations! They could build up over the three weeks a complete 'strip cartoon' of the whole story, to be used in introducing the theme in all-age worship. The pictures could be on a continuous frieze, or on cardboard placards held on poles by the children, or separate pictures fixed around the walls before the service starts. Children could enter at different points as the story is told, holding their placard, or – well, you think of your own ideas – they'll probably be better than mine, anyway.

Drama

The dramatised version of the story is included. It can simply be used as a dramatised reading, with different children literally reading the parts, or it could be developed if your group has a flair for it into something much bigger. Adapt it freely to suit your group. If you need more parts, try splitting the narrator's part between several children, or add in one or two new characters. During the free discussion of the story things might emerge that it would be good to include in the dialogue. Feel free to photocopy these pages and make your own alterations if you wish. The drama can then either be used simply as a teaching aid or rehearsed and presented in the all-age worship. An added touch might be to use a domestic tape recorder to record it – then each child could take home a recording of a play with their own voice on it!

Worksheet

This is included for you to use as you see fit. You could have some of the children colour in the pictures and display them at the service, or you could let a group work through the sheet as part of the session; or it could simply be given to them as a take-home sheet to help them remember the session and/or to share with their families.

All-age worship

This is the culmination of the unit, but please don't allow preparation for it to dominate and spoil the sessions. It's not a performance, and no one will mind if what the children produce isn't beautifully polished – the main thing is that they should be seen to be enjoying it.

The services are designed to be truly 'all-age', involving the whole congregation, and – most importantly – giving opportunities for interaction across the age groups. There are no 'children's talks', but rather all-age activities.

This approach needs to be reflected in the overall balance of the service, so that it is one in which all people can participate rather than a children's service with the adults as indulgent spectators.

Let's take a look at the various elements:

Songs

Naturally, there will be songs specifically chosen by the children, or at least with them in mind. But including some more 'adult' hymns not only shows respect to the older worshippers but also requires the children to sample a more varied diet and hopefully broaden their taste.

Welcome and statement of the theme

An example is given, but please feel free to use your own words and adapt it for your own circumstances. It's an important element in the service, for it introduces the chosen theme and sets it in the wider context. It is also a jolly good opportunity to point out some of the creative work the children have done, and have it suitably acknowledged by the congregation.

Prayers

Again, an opening prayer is offered, but it's not mandatory! Local worship leaders will probably want to do something more appropriate to the particular setting.

Word and action

The Bible story selected from one of the weeks 1-3 is not only read but reinforced with an all-age activity. The essential point is to make this at once meaningful and enjoyable. If people enjoy it, they're far more likely to enter into it. One important point, though: you know your own congregation best, and are in a position to ensure that people aren't treated insensitively. If you know that Mrs X doesn't like being in the limelight, then avoid drawing attention to her. Finally, watch the time. People will warm to the subject and be difficult to stop! You will also then be deluged with responses, many of them duplicated in different groups. Keep the discussion short and to the point, and move on. And don't forget to consider setting up the action group (see Introduction, page 7) – people need to know this isn't just a talking shop!

Offertory prayer

All we do and give is a free response to what God does for and gives to us. The offertory prayer is a good opportunity to highlight that point. This helps to avoid religion becoming 'works centred' rather than being a free, joyful response to God's grace.

Reading

Because you're using imaginatively rewritten stories, it's very important to read from a standard Bible in the service, and this point should never be overlooked. Children – and especially the older ones and the young people – need to hear the Bible read and come to appreciate it for themselves.

Talk

It's marked 'optional', but it's actually quite an important part of the service. As with the Bible, the traditional sermon is too valuable (when done well) to throw away. In a service of this nature, a short talk helps develop and maintain the skills of listening and reasoning. Keep it short, though, or it will have the opposite effect! On the other hand, if the service is running over time, this is an element that could *occasionally* be omitted.

Notices and family news

All too often, notices are regarded as an intrusion, and ways are often found to 'get them out of the way'. But surely, this is the life of the Church that is being shared here – and should it not be offered to God, along with the lives of his people? In the service order, I've suggested putting the notices directly before the Intercessions, so they can then feed into the prayers, thus integrating them more closely into the worship.

This is also a suitable time to do something else – the 'Family News'. People who have, for example, a birthday, or a wedding anniversary, or perhaps who are changing jobs, retiring or whatever, can share that with the congregation. A supply of cards can be kept in the church, with a suitably general message in them, to be handed out to people along with the good wishes and applause of the congregation. This is one slot we daren't leave out at Anstey, or we hear about it!

Intercessions

If Jesus was 'the man for others', it's hard to imagine worship that is genuinely Christian and doesn't include some sort of intercession for others. You will certainly want to include some of the children's own concerns that have emerged in the sessions in these prayers. You might also want to use some of the artwork to help the congregation focus on particular things. Whoever leads these, try to ensure that they are done thoughtfully, with a concern for the whole of God's creation, and not just Christians.

Closing prayer/benediction

Another element that should be kept short but meaningful! This is where the congregation are sent out into the world to live in some way the values and ideals they have expressed in their worship.

Now, go to it!

Most importantly of all – use the material imaginatively; make it work *for you*. It is your servant, not your director. What matters is that all involved enjoy the sessions, learn about valuing and being valued, build relationships with each other and with 'staff', and learn along the way.

That's how Jesus worked whenever he could. And it's not a bad example to follow!

Unit 1
The Law – Moses

Overview of the Unit

Theme: God is here in the unexpected

We take three key events:

Week 1: Moses in the bulrushes

Moses is born into an Israelite slave family in Egypt, hidden in a basket in the bulrushes and discovered by an Egyptian princess who brings him up as her own – and unwittingly employs his mother as his nurse!

Week 2: The Passover

The Israelite slaves are liberated from Egypt, but at a terrible human cost – and they begin their long journey to freedom.

Week 3: God gives Moses the Ten Commandments

Moses finds that keeping free people in order is a real headache, and God gives him the Ten Commandments.

All-age worship

Here, you may choose to focus on any one of the three sub-themes, but place it in the context of the overall story of Moses. So while the specific theme chosen will be emphasised in the choice of 'Word and action' material, some of the art and craft work the children have done in the other weeks will be used to decorate the church and set the context of the wider story.

Important note

✔ The ticked activities in Weeks 1-3 are intended as the link material for the 'Word and action' slot in the all-age worship. You will only need to do this in one of the three weeks – depending on which week's sub-theme is going to be the main emphasis in the service.

Week 1: Moses in the bulrushes

Thinking about it

What's the point?

This is real undercover stuff! God doesn't call in the cavalry from outside, but creates hope within the situation. His liberator is born as one of the slaves and then infiltrates the royal household itself.

Doing it

Prayer

Loving God,
thank you for being with us,
when things are good and when they're not.
Help us, together, to learn to trust you and each other more.
Amen.

From the known to the unknown

Before the session, conceal some of the session materials – crayons, felt-tip pens, for example – around the room. Then ask the children to help you find them, so that the session can begin. Sometimes, when God gives us the things we need, he doesn't make them obvious – we have to search for them. The Israelites needed a leader to set them free, and God gave them one – but he had to be hidden away until the time was right.

Tell the story: Exodus 1:22-2:10

(See page 20 for a dramatised version of this story.)

Cunning plans

Imagine that you have a new baby in the family – and he's in great danger. You must hide him before the wicked king can get to him. Any ideas?

Well, let me take you to a land far away, and a time long ago. The evil king, Pharaoh, is hatching a horrible plan. 'These Israelites,' he says, 'I hate them. Why couldn't they have stayed in their own country? They're going to take over all of Egypt, that's what. Well, I'm going to stop them.'

Of course, everybody listens – they all want to know what cunning plan Pharaoh has for getting rid of all the foreign people in Egypt. 'Kill all the boy babies,' he says. 'If there aren't enough men, they won't be able to fight me, will they? Then I can do exactly what I want.'

Meanwhile, in a little shack, an Israelite mother has just had a baby – and it's a boy. 'What are we going to do?' she says. 'If the king finds out, he'll have him killed!' Well, the first three months are OK – they just keep him well hidden and nobody knows he's there. But it can't go on, can it?

'It's no good,' Mum says. 'We're going to have to find somewhere else to hide him.' And that's when she gets the most amazing idea.

'We'll make him a basket out of reeds,' she says, 'and we'll seal it with tar so it'll float – and we can hide it among the rushes at the side of the river.'

Her daughter, Miriam, thinks she's really lost it! 'Mother, you're mad!' she tells her. 'What if something horrible happens to him? What if he drowns?'

'Ah, but he won't,' Mother answers. 'Because you'll be watching – won't you!'

So, that's how Miriam ends up hiding in the bushes near the River Nile, watching a basket hidden in the rushes. Then something terrible happens: somebody comes for a swim. And that somebody isn't just anybody, it's a princess body! This is the daughter of the king – the same king who's frightened of foreigners and wants to kill all their babies! She goes into the river, and, of course, she sees the basket. 'Hey, you – servant-person!' she calls to her maid. 'Get me that basket, so I can see what's in it.'

Of course, Miriam's shaking like a leaf, in the bushes, thinking that her little brother's for the chop at any moment. The princess opens the basket and looks in.

'It's a baby boy!' she says. 'Hey, I bet it's one of those Israelite babies. I bet the mother's hidden it to try and fool my dad.'

Miriam's really worried now, of course – but she can't do anything. Suddenly, the princess smiles!

'Well, yippy skip for her!' she says. 'It's about time one of them put one over on old Dad – he's been getting worse, you know, but don't tell him I said that. Tell you what, let's take him home.'

Naturally, the maid's a bit alarmed at this. 'Take him home?' she echoes. 'Have you gone mad – er, Your Royal Highness? What'll the king do?'

'Oh, he'll never notice,' the princess says. 'One more child in the palace will be neither here nor there. Let's go.'

Well, Miriam's got to think fast, hasn't she! Before she's had time to work out all the details, she's on her feet, calling to the princess.

'Um, excuse me, Your, er, Gloriousness – I couldn't help overhearing – just sitting in the bushes counting butterflies, the way you do – but I know a slave who'd make a really good nanny.'

Naturally, the princess is a bit taken aback at first – it's not every day she's shouted at from the bushes while she's having a swim and kidnapping a baby. 'Oh, OK then – sounds a good idea,' she answers.

So there's Miriam, running like she's never run before, to get her mum.

'Hey, Mum – they've found him – but it's OK – he's going to be a prince – and they want you to be his nanny.'

Meanwhile, the princess is thinking, 'What are we going to call him? He's got to have a name of some sort. I know – I'll call him Moses, because I brought him out of the water.'*

---

* No one's absolutely sure what the connection is, but there's a word in the language of the Bible that's quite like 'Moses' and means 'to bring out'. Moses was brought out of the water, and God was going to use him to bring his people out of Egypt. Good, eh!

So it all ends up with Moses being taken to the royal household, right under Pharaoh's nose, and completely behind his back – if you see what I mean – to be brought up by his own mother who everyone thinks is his nanny. And that's just the beginning, folks.

Respond to the story

Discussion

Why did Moses' mother hide him away in the bulrushes?

- to get a bit of peace and quiet?
- to play a game with wicked old Pharaoh?
- because she loved him and wanted him to be safe?

How do the children think she felt when the princess found him, and asked her to be his nanny?

- frightened?
- nervous?
- glad he was safe?
- Pleased that she could look after him again?

Song

One or more of the following songs might be used here and/or in the all-age worship:

One more step along the world I go
Special agents, we're special agents
There are hundreds of sparrows (God knows me)
When there is nowhere to turn

Art and craft

✔ Make a reed bed from drinking straws. (See 'Word and action' in the all-age worship for how this would be used.) Blu-Tack or tape several good-sized pieces of oasis to a table top and push the straws into it. You could paint the straws to make them resemble rushes, and if you have the time and resources to be really creative, you could add paper fronds to make them more realistic. Then prepare some cards – probably about half as big as postcards – for writing on. Depending on just how you are using this idea, you might need just a few or enough for every worshipper to have one.

Draw or paint a picture of Moses in his basket in the bulrushes.

This is the key picture, but you might want to do others in addition to it, such as:

- the princess coming to the river to bathe
- Miriam running to get her mother
- Moses' mother holding him, in the palace

Drama

See the next page for a dramatised version of the story.

Drama: Cunning plans

Narrator	Imagine that you have a new baby in the family – and he's in great danger. You must hide him before the wicked king can get to him. Any ideas? Well, let me take you to a land far away, and a time long ago. The evil king, Pharaoh, is hatching a horrible plan.
Pharaoh	These Israelites, I hate them. Why couldn't they have stayed in their own country? They're going to take over all of Egypt, that's what. Well, I'm going to stop them.
Narrator	Of course, everybody listens – they all want to know what cunning plan Pharaoh has for getting rid of all the foreign people in Egypt.
Pharaoh	Kill all the boy babies. If there aren't enough men, they won't be able to fight me, will they? Then I can do exactly what I want.
Narrator	Meanwhile, in a little shack, an Israelite mother has just had a baby – and it's a boy.
Mother	What are we going to do? If the king finds out he'll have him killed!
Narrator	Well, the first three months are OK – they just keep him well hidden and nobody knows he's there. But it can't go on, can it?
Mother	It's no good, we're going to have to find somewhere else to hide him.
Narrator	And that's when she gets the most amazing idea.
Mother	We'll make him a basket out of reeds, and we'll seal it with tar so it'll float – and we can hide it among the rushes at the side of the river.
Narrator	Her daughter, Miriam, thinks she's really lost it!
Miriam	Mother, you're mad! What if something horrible happens to him? What if he drowns?
Mother	Ah, but he won't. Because you'll be watching – won't you!
Narrator	So, that's how Miriam ends up hiding in the bushes near the River Nile, watching a basket hidden in the rushes. Then something terrible happens: somebody comes for a swim. And that somebody isn't just anybody, it's a princess body! This is the daughter of the king – the same king who's frightened of foreigners and wants to kill all their babies! She goes into the river, and, of course, she sees the basket.
Princess	Hey, you – servant-person! Get me that basket, so I can see what's in it.
Maid	Yes, Your Highness.
Narrator	Of course, Miriam's shaking like a leaf, in the bushes, thinking that her little brother's for the chop at any moment. The princess opens the basket and looks in.
Princess	It's a baby boy! Hey, I bet it's one of those Israelite babies. I bet the mother's hidden it to try and fool my dad.

Narrator	Miriam's really worried now, of course – but she can't do anything. Suddenly, the princess smiles!
Princess	Well, yippy skip for her! It's about time one of them put one over on old Dad – he's been getting worse, you know, but don't tell him I said that. Tell you what, let's take him home.
Narrator	Naturally, the maid's a bit alarmed at this.
Maid	Take him home? Have you gone mad – er, Your Royal Highness? What'll the king do?
Princess	Oh, he'll never notice. One more child in the palace will be neither here nor there. Let's go.
Narrator	Well, Miriam's got to think fast, hasn't she! Before she's had time to work out all the details, she's on her feet, calling to the princess.
Miriam	Um, excuse me, Your, er, Gloriousness – I couldn't help over-hearing – just sitting in the bushes counting butterflies, the way you do – but I know a slave who'd make a really good nanny.
Narrator	Naturally, the princess is a bit taken aback at first – it's not every day she gets shouted at from the bushes while she's having a swim and kidnapping a baby.
Princess	Oh, OK, then – sounds a good idea.
Narrator	So there's Miriam, running like she's never run before, to get her mum.
Miriam	Hey, Mum – they've found him – but it's OK – he's going to be a prince – and they want you to be his nanny.
Princess	Now, what are we going to call him? He's got to have a name of some sort. I know – I'll call him Moses, because I brought him out of the water.
Narrator	So it all ends up with Moses being taken to the royal household, right under Pharaoh's nose, and completely behind his back – if you see what I mean – to be brought up by his own mother who everyone thinks is his nanny. And that's just the beginning, folks.

Miriam is watching Moses carefully. Can you find her?

These pictures may look the same,
but can you spot 7 differences?

WORDSEARCH

Find the following words
in the grid:

MOSES, BASKET, RUSHES,
RIVER, PHARAOH, EGYPT,
ISRAELITE, MIRIAM,
PRINCESS, NANNY

```
S B P R I N C E S S T V
E G Y I H O A R A H P D
S T R V X G S E H S U R
U M I R I A M O S E G I
M O S L P H A R A G E V
I S R A E N A N N Y C E
B R I N C A S K E P S R
N A N N X N R U S T Y S
R U S H E N I S R A E G
B A S K E Y P R I S R A
P R I N E S S M O S A S
I S R A E T P M G E B S
```

Week 2: The Passover

Thinking about it

What's the point?

All of us, in one way or another, are slaves. When God sets us free, it's most often a call to journey with him – a journey not only of liberation but of discovery.

Doing it

Prayer

Thank you, God, for our freedom.
Thank you that we are free to be here today.
Help us to show your love to one another.
Amen.

From the known to the unknown

Ask the children to remember memorable journeys they've undertaken – perhaps to a holiday destination. Was the journey just a way of getting where they were going, or was it worthwhile in itself? Did they, for example, see wonderful views from an aeroplane, or travel by road through new places? Did they even, maybe, learn things?

Faith in God is like a journey: we don't get it all at once – in fact, the journey never really ends!

Tell the story: Exodus 7:14-12:42

(See page 26 for a dramatised version of this story.)

God sets his people free

Today we're in ancient Egypt again. Moses has grown up, and God's chosen him for a very special job. 'You're going to set my people free,' he's told Moses. 'The Israelites are not going to be slaves any more, because I'm going to lead them to a land of their own. Now, you go and tell Pharaoh that.'

Now, Pharaoh, the wicked King of Egypt, isn't the kind of person you tell what to do – but Moses can probably get away with it, because he knows him. But he really has to twist Pharaoh's arm all the same. 'If you don't stop ill-treating God's people,' he says, 'God's going to make your life really horrible.'

Well, of course, Pharaoh doesn't believe in the God of Moses, so he just laughs at him – until the plagues start. God and Moses try everything. God shows his power by turning the river water to blood, but Pharaoh won't give in. God fills the country with frogs, and then there are gnats and flies – getting into everything they are, crawling all over people's dinner, hiding in their clothes – but Pharaoh still says no. Then the animals all die, and the people get boils, but Pharaoh refuses to take notice. Then the big storms start – hail and lightning like you've never seen – and after that comes the great darkness – darkness so thick you can feel it. And still Pharaoh won't budge. 'Get out of my sight!' he yells at Moses. 'If ever I see you again, you're dead. Got it?'

So God speaks to Moses again. 'Right,' he says, 'I hoped I wouldn't have to do this, but we're really going to have to hit Pharaoh hard to make him let my people go. Tell the Israelites to hold special dinners in their homes. They're to eat lamb, and before they cook it they've got to put some of its blood on the door of their homes – because at midnight I'm going to bring death to every Egyptian household – but the houses with the lambs' blood on them will be safely passed over. Now, make sure they all do it – OK?'

Well, what can Moses say? 'OK, God – you're the boss.'

But God isn't finished yet. 'Now,' he says, 'the bread for the meal – don't use any yeast in it because you haven't time for all that palaver. Things are really happening now. You're all to be dressed ready for a journey – shoes, outdoor clothes, walking sticks, the lot – because I'm not going to be hanging around. And from now on, you'll celebrate this day every year as a festival, because this is the night I'm setting you free.'

Well, the people are amazed. 'Bread without yeast?' the women say. 'We're proud of our bread, we are – what's it going to be like if we don't do it properly?'

But Moses insists. 'No yeast – no time!' he says. 'Hats and coats on, shoes on your feet, and whatever you do, don't forget the blood on the door.'

So there they are – around the dinner tables in their homes, with the blood painted on the doors, eating their roast lamb and this strange bread made without yeast – and the angel of death passes over the houses, looking for the Egyptian homes. Suddenly, there's terrible wailing and crying. Every Egyptian house has someone who's been killed – and in the cowsheds and chicken pens, as well, some of the animals die. Even the eldest son of the King of Egypt himself doesn't escape.

Well, that does it! The king calls for Moses and his brother Aaron. 'Get out of my country!' he bellows at them. 'I don't want anything more to do with you, or your people, or your terrible God!'

So the Israelites don't waste any time. They've already got their coats and hats on, they've got shoes on their feet and walking sticks in their hands, and they've a supply of dough to make that funny instant bread, so they won't starve in the desert. So they're up and off, with their children, their animals and whatever they can carry on the journey.

Through the streets they walk, toward the border of Egypt, and, all the way, Egyptians are coming out of their houses and urging them on. They're not just letting their slaves go – they're positively begging them to! Then they reach the border and walk across it. They're free! No more slaving in the hot sun while the Egyptians have a siesta, no more being beaten for not working hard enough, no more chains and whips and insults about being Israelites. They're free – free to be God's own people!

They look around, and where do you think they are? The Promised Land? Or maybe a beautiful garden? Or possibly a holiday camp with lots to eat and to do? Nothing like that at all: they're in a desert. Nothing but sand for miles and miles. 'How are we going to find our way across that?' they say. 'Where's this land of our own God promised us? What about all the milk and honey we were expecting to find?'

'Oh, don't worry, God's going to get us there,' Moses tells them. 'This isn't the end of the story – it's just the beginning of the most exciting journey of all time!'

Respond to the story

Discussion

What do the children think the slaves were expecting when God said he'd set them free?

- a ride on a magic carpet?
- to be 'beamed' to their new home in an instant?

Why do the children think God didn't do those things, since we may fairly assume that he could have done them? Why did he choose to lead them on a journey?

- to give them time to learn about him?
- to give them time to grow from a rabble into a nation?
- to give them the choice of following him, not just force them?

Song

One or more of the following songs might be used here and/or in the all-age worship:

One more step along the world I go
The Spirit lives to set us free (Walk, walk in the light)
We are marching in the light of God
We need to grow, grow, grow, grow

Art and craft

✔ Make some paper chains. (See 'Word and action' in the all-age worship for how this would be used.) You could use ready-made strips of paper bought from a shop, or let the children cut up and colour their own strips, using sticky tape to close the links. You will need enough chains for the number of groups you anticipate dividing the Sunday congregation into, and each with at least half a dozen links. Make sure you have some balloons ready to attach to the chains on Sunday. (Explain to the children that you're making 'ball and chain' sets of the kind prisoners and slaves once used to wear, because you're going to be thinking about slavery in the Sunday service.)

Draw or paint a picture of Passover (perhaps of the table set for the meal, or of people in overcoats sitting down to eat), and/or make some 'unleavened bread' from modelling clay, explaining to the children as they work that the Israelites didn't use yeast because they were people in a hurry and it wouldn't have time to rise – so the 'loaves' are going to be quite flat.

These are the key images, but you might want to do others in addition to them, such as:

- Pictures of the desert – a daunting sight at the start of a journey!
- Pictures of each of the plagues – they could be put up in order in the church.

Drama: God sets his people free

Narrator	Today, we're in ancient Egypt again. Moses has grown up, and God's chosen him for a very special job.
God	Moses? God here. You're going to set my people free. The Israelites are not going to be slaves any more, because I'm going to lead them to a land of their own. Now, you go and tell Pharaoh that.
Narrator	Now, Pharaoh, the wicked King of Egypt, isn't the kind of person you tell what to do – but Moses can probably get away with it, because he knows him. But he really has to twist Pharaoh's arm, all the same.
Moses	If you don't stop ill-treating God's people, God's going to make your life really horrible – er, Your Majesty.
Narrator	Well, of course, Pharaoh doesn't believe in the God of Moses, so he just laughs at him – until the plagues start. God and Moses try everything. God shows his power by turning the river water to blood, but Pharaoh won't give in. God fills the country with frogs, and then there are gnats and flies – getting into everything, they are, crawling all over people's dinner, hiding in their clothes – but Pharaoh still says no.
Pharaoh	I'm still saying no.
Narrator	Then the animals all die, and the people get boils, but Pharaoh refuses to take notice.
Pharaoh	I'm refusing to take notice.
Narrator	Then the big storms start – hail and lightning like you've never seen – and after that comes the great darkness – darkness so thick you can feel it. And still Pharaoh won't budge. He just gets angry.
Pharaoh	Get out of my sight, Moses. If ever I see you again, you're dead. Got it?
Narrator	So God speaks to Moses again.
God	Right. I hoped I wouldn't have to do this, but we're really going to have to hit Pharaoh hard to make him let my people go. Tell the Israelites to hold special dinners in their homes. They're to eat lamb, and before they cook it they've got to put some of its blood on the door of their homes – because at midnight I'm going to bring death to every Egyptian household – but the houses with the lambs' blood on them will be safely passed over. Now, make sure they all do it – OK?
Moses	OK, God – you're the boss.
God	Now, the bread for the meal – don't use any yeast in it because you haven't time for all that palaver. Things are really happening now. You're all to be dressed ready for a journey – shoes, outdoor clothes, walking sticks, the lot – because I'm not going to be hanging around. And from now on, you'll celebrate

this day every year as a festival, because this is the night I'm setting you free.

Narrator   Well, the people are amazed.

Woman 1   Bread without yeast? We can't do that!

Woman 2   We're proud of our bread, we are – what's it going to be like if we don't do it properly?

Moses   No yeast. We haven't time! Hats and coats on, shoes on your feet, and whatever you do, don't forget the blood on the door.

Narrator   So there they are – around the dinner tables in their homes, wearing their outdoor clothes, with the blood painted on the doors, eating their roast lamb and this strange bread made without yeast – and the angel of death passes over the houses, looking for the Egyptian homes. Suddenly, there's terrible wailing and crying. In every Egyptian house the eldest child has been killed – and even in the cowsheds and chicken pens, as well, some of the animals die. Even the eldest son of the King of Egypt himself doesn't escape. Well, that does it! The king calls for Moses and his brother Aaron.

Pharaoh   Get out of my country! I don't want anything more to do with you, or your people, or your terrible God!

Narrator   So the Israelites don't waste any time. They've already got their coats and hats on, they've got shoes on their feet and walking sticks in their hands, and they've a supply of dough to make that funny instant bread, so they won't starve in the desert. So they're up and off, with their children, their animals and whatever they can carry on the journey. As they walk, Egyptians are coming out of their houses and urging them on. They're not just letting their slaves go – they're positively begging them to! Then they get to the border, and walk across it. They're free! No more slaving in the hot sun while the Egyptians have a siesta, no more being beaten for not working hard enough, no more chains and whips and insults about being Israelites. They're free – free to be God's own people! They look around, and where do you think they are? In a desert, that's where. Nothing but sand for miles and miles.

Woman 1   How are we going to find our way across that?

Woman 2   Where's this land of our own God promised us? What about all the milk and honey we were expecting to find?

Moses   Oh, don't worry, God's going to get us there. This isn't the end of the story – it's just the beginning of the most exciting journey of all time!

Colour this picture, using crayon, paint or felt-tips

Passover

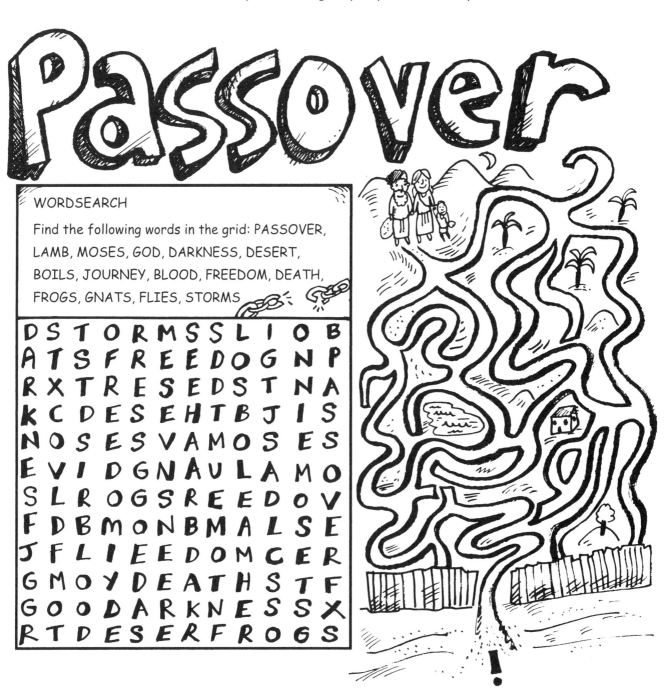

WORDSEARCH

Find the following words in the grid: PASSOVER, LAMB, MOSES, GOD, DARKNESS, DESERT, BOILS, JOURNEY, BLOOD, FREEDOM, DEATH, FROGS, GNATS, FLIES, STORMS

```
D S T O R M S S L I O B
A T S F R E E D O G N P
R X T R E S E D S T N A
K C D E S E H T B J I S
N O S E S V A M O S E S
E V I D G N A U L A M O
S L R O G S R E E D O V
F D B M O N B M A L S E
J F L I E E D O M C E R
G M O Y D E A T H S T F
G O O D A R K N E S S X
R T D E S E R F R O G S
```

Get the Israelites to the border and out of Egypt

28

Week 3: The Ten Commandments

Thinking about it

What's the point?

Freedom isn't the same as anarchy – none of us can be truly free if we don't feel safe. We need structure and a basic framework for living. So God's law is intended to set us free – not make us into slaves again!

Doing it

Prayer

Thank you, God,
for this time and place where we can be free.
Help us to use our freedom well,
so that friendship grows and everyone benefits.
Amen.

From the known to the unknown

Have the children ever felt frightened because no one seemed to be in charge? Perhaps it was a situation in a school playground, or in a busy street. Do you have your own story of that kind to share? Keep this activity light-hearted – just a few quick examples. We all need some kind of structure – to feel that we have a safe framework for our lives.

Tell the story: Exodus 18:13-20:17

(See page 32 for a dramatised version of this story.)

Rules for free people

OK, the Israelites have left Egypt, so they're not slaves any more, and they're on their way to the land God's promised them. Moses is the one God's chosen to lead them – and what do you think he's spending all his time doing? Settling arguments, that's what. They just can't stop wrangling among themselves, and then Moses has to sort it out. His father-in-law, Jethro, notices. 'Hey, what's going on?' he says. 'Why are you spending your time settling quarrels – with long queues of people waiting around all day to see you when they should have work to do?'

'Someone's got to,' says Moses. 'When they have a quarrel, I tell them who's right.'

Jethro thinks Moses is doing it the hard way, and tells him so. 'You need help,' he says. 'Why not appoint judges to do this for you? You can tell everyone what God's rules are, and then the judges will be able to decide who's right and who's wrong. Of course, they can still bring the really difficult arguments to you, but you won't be worn out, and they'll get sorted.'

Well, that sounds good to Moses, so he does it – appoints lots of judges to settle people's arguments. But, hang on a minute – if you've got judges, you need laws, don't you?

Now, as it happens, the Israelites are camped near a big mountain, called Mount Sinai – so Moses hoofs it up the mountain to get a bit of peace and quiet and listen to God.

It's really spooky. Thick clouds and smoke – because God's chosen to show himself to Moses in fire.* So it's dark, hot, and no place to be if you've got asthma.

'This is our place,' God says to Moses, 'yours and mine. The rest of the people can wait expectantly at the bottom of the hill. *Are* the people waiting expectantly?'

'Oh, yes, Lord,' Moses assures him, 'they're all waiting. Expectantly.'

'Then you'd better go back down and make sure they don't get any big ideas and start to follow you,' God tells him. 'And while you're down there, you can fetch your brother Aaron and bring him up here to me.'

So Moses has to go all the way back down, give them the message, and then bring Aaron back up the mountain. Then God lays down the law. 'I'm God,' he says, 'and don't you forget it. Remember *I* set you free, and don't go worshipping other gods, because it won't do you any good. OK?'

'OK, God, you're the boss,' Moses and Aaron say.

'Good,' says God. 'And I don't want you making statues to worship, either. Oh, yes, I know it goes on, but I'm too great to be represented by a statue – or a picture, come to that – so it's me you're going to worship. And another thing: don't use my name in bad ways.'

Moses and Aaron aren't too sure what that means. 'You mean, like using it as a swear word?'

'Yes, and other things, too,' God tells them.† 'Anyway, moving on: have a special day for rest and worship – a holy day when you can listen to me, and think about other things that are really important – and yes, I know you do that every day, but once a week you can make a point of it. Got it?'

'Oh, yes, God,' Moses and Aaron say, 'we've got it.'

'Good,' God says. 'Now, that's about you and me. I've got some more rules, and they're about you and each other. And it all starts with respect – respect your parents, because that's your first step to long life and happiness in the new land I'm giving you. And respect for others is what it's all about really – like, if you respect people, you won't kill them, will you? Husbands and wives won't cheat on one another, and you won't take things that don't belong to you – no, not even to borrow, unless you ask first.'

Aaron looks a bit embarrassed at this. 'You know that hammer you lost, Moses? Well, I'll give it back to you when we get home.'

'Moving quickly on,' God continues, 'just a couple more. Don't tell lies about people. And don't come that "sticks and stones" rubbish with me, either. Words *do* hurt – and gossip ruins lives. So don't do it. OK?'

---

* Can the children think of another time when God showed himself to Moses in fire? It's not in this book, but some of them may know.

† Like what? Any ideas? (What about being dishonest when we know people will trust us because we're Christians – would that be one? Or, perhaps, saying, 'God has told me this', just to get our own way?)

'OK, God – you're the boss.'

'Now,' says God, 'if you want to be really safe, "Don't do it" isn't enough. It's "Don't even think about it". Don't even *think* about wanting things other people have got – whether it's gismos, goats, gadgets or girlfriends. And the same goes for boyfriends, too. Now, tell the people to keep those ten rules and they won't go far wrong.'

'Oh, yes,' says Aaron, 'we'll all keep them all the time.'

Well, if they had, they might have got on a little better. But we all know how hard keeping the rules can be, don't we?

Respond to the story

Discussion

Why do the children think God decided to give the Israelites some rules?

- to stop them enjoying themselves?
- to give them some guidelines for living?
- to help them use their freedom well and be happy?

It might be helpful to ask the children for some examples of rules they find helpful and rules they don't, and briefly discuss them.

Song

One or more of the following songs might be used here and/or in the all-age worship:

A new commandment
Jesus, reign in me
Lord, the light of your love is shining
Obey the maker's instructions

Art and craft

✔ Make something to represent a prison cell. (See 'Word and action' in the all-age worship for how this would be used.) This could be as simple as a barred window cut from cardboard, for the prisoner to hold in front of his or her face, or you could beg some large cardboard boxes from a removal company and use these to make a complete cell – or go for various stages in between. As you work, remind the children of the earlier discussion, and ask them to imagine a world where there were no laws and everyone could do just as they liked. Pretty frightening? In a world like that they'd need somewhere to hide away – and that's what you're making. Now, you need a volunteer to go into the cell during the service and refuse to come out because they don't trust the congregation – if they want to give one or two reasons – such as 'They don't like City supporters' – that's fine, but keep it light-hearted.

Draw or paint a picture of Moses up the mountain – don't forget the fire and thick smoke!

This is the key picture, but you might want to do others in addition to it, such as:

- Moses acting as judge for the people
- scales of justice
- stone tablets with the ten commandments written on them

Drama: Rules for free people

Narrator	OK, the Israelites have left Egypt, so they're not slaves any more, and they're on their way to the land God's promised them. Moses is the one God's chosen to lead them – and what d'you think he's spending all his time doing? Settling arguments, that's what. They just can't stop wrangling among themselves, and then Moses has to sort it out. His father-in-law, Jethro, notices.
Jethro	Hey, what's going on, Moses? Why are you spending your time settling quarrels – with long queues of people waiting around all day to see you when they should have work to do?
Moses	Someone's got to. When they have a quarrel, I tell them who's right.
Jethro	You need help. Why not appoint judges to do this for you? You can tell everyone what God's rules are, and then the judges will be able to decide who's right and who's wrong. Of course, they can still bring the really difficult arguments to you, but you won't be worn out, and they'll get sorted.
Narrator	Well, that sounds good to Moses, so he does it – appoints lots of judges to settle people's arguments. But, hang on a minute – if you've got judges, you need laws, don't you? Now, as it happens, the Israelites are camped near a big mountain, called Mount Sinai – so Moses hoofs it up the mountain to get a bit of peace and quiet and listen to God. It's really spooky. Thick clouds and smoke – because God's chosen to show himself to Moses in fire. So it's dark, hot, and no place to be if you've got asthma. But God hasn't – so he can talk freely.
God	This is our place, Moses, yours and mine. The rest of the people can wait expectantly at the bottom of the hill. *Are* the people waiting expectantly?
Moses	Oh, yes, Lord, they're all waiting. Expectantly.
God	Then you'd better go back down and make sure they don't get any big ideas and start to follow you. And while you're down there, you can fetch you brother Aaron and bring him up here to me.
Narrator	So Moses has to go all the way back down, give them the message, and then bring Aaron back up the mountain. Then God lays down the law.
God	I'm God, and don't you forget it. Remember *I* set you free, and don't go worshipping other gods, because it won't do you any good. OK?
Moses	OK, God.
Aaron	You're the boss.
God	Good. And I don't want you making statues to worship, either. Oh, yes, I know it goes on, but I'm too great to be represented by a statue – or a picture, come to that – so it's me you're

going to worship. And another thing: don't use my name in bad ways.

Moses   Like, how, exactly?

Aaron   You mean, like using it as a swear word?

God   Yes, and other things, too.*

Anyway, moving on: have a special day for rest and worship – a holy day when you can listen to me, and think about other things that are really important – and yes, I know you do that every day, but once a week you can make a point of it. Got it?

Moses   Oh, yes, God.

Aaron   We've got it.

God   Good. Now, that's about you and me. I've got some more rules, and they're about you and each other. And it all starts with respect – respect your parents, because that's your first step to long life and happiness in the new land I'm giving you. And respect for others is what it's all about really – like, if you respect people, you won't kill them, will you? Husbands and wives won't cheat on one another, and you won't take things that don't belong to you – no, not even to borrow, unless you ask first.

Aaron   You know that hammer you lost, Moses? Well, I'll give it back to you when we get home.

God   Moving quickly on, just a couple more. Don't tell lies about people. And don't come that 'sticks and stones' rubbish with me, either. Words *do* hurt – and gossip ruins lives. So don't do it. OK? And finally, if you want to be really safe, 'Don't do it' isn't enough. It's 'Don't even think about it'. Don't even think about wanting things other people have got – whether it's gismos, goats, gadgets or girlfriends. And, girls: the same goes for boyfriends, too. Now, tell the people to keep those ten rules and they won't go far wrong.

* Can the children think of any examples to write into God's speech, here? (If you need a little help, see the footnote in the narrative version.)

33

Moses has lost his hammer – can you help him find it?

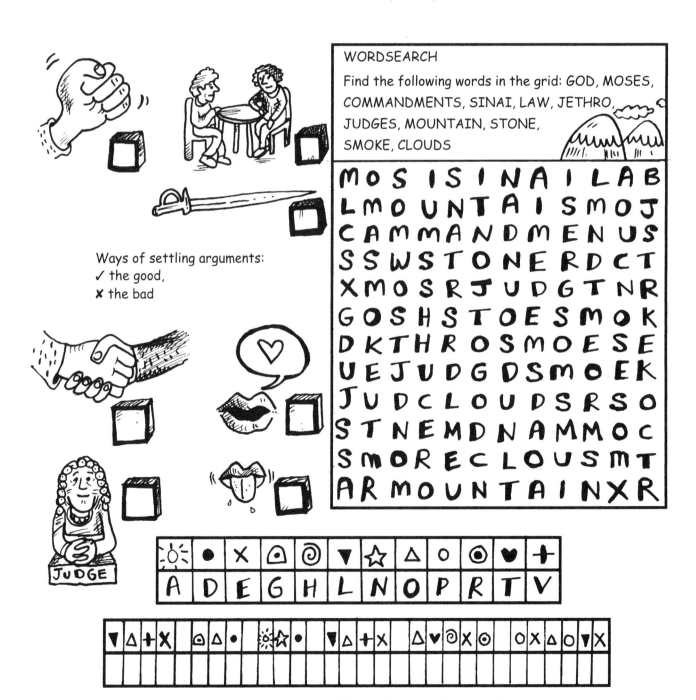

WORDSEARCH

Find the following words in the grid: GOD, MOSES, COMMANDMENTS, SINAI, LAW, JETHRO, JUDGES, MOUNTAIN, STONE, SMOKE, CLOUDS

```
M O S I S I N A I L A B
L M O U N T A I S M O J
C A M M A N D M E N U S
S S W S T O N E R D C T
X M O S R J U D G T N R
G O S H S T O E S M O K
D K T H R O S M O E S E
U E J U D G D S M O E K
J U D C L O U D S R S O
S T N E M D N A M M O C
S M O R E C L O U S M T
A R M O U N T A I N X R
```

Ways of settling arguments:
✓ the good,
✗ the bad

Crack the code to find all God's laws neatly summed up

Week 4: All-age worship

Opening song

> A song praising and celebrating the faithfulness of God

Welcome and statement of the theme

> Get one or more of the children to point out or hold up the pictures as you sum up the story:

> In Junior Church during the past few weeks, we've been learning about Moses who traditionally represents the Law. We learnt how he was born as one of the Israelite slaves in Egypt, and how he was hidden away in the bulrushes by his family but discovered by an Egyptian princess who brought him up as her own child. So for Israel, God's hope didn't come from outside, but was hidden within the situation. Then we read about the Passover, when God told the Israelites to eat their celebration meal with their outdoor clothes on – we got a sense of urgency from that, as if God is asking us always to be ready to move on when he calls us. Finally, we read about how Moses and the people learned that free people need structure and discipline – so God gave them the ten commandments to help them make the most of their freedom.

> That's the general picture, but today we're going to concentrate on: [*Name the episode of your choice*]

Prayer – use whichever is appropriate

Based on Week 1

> Loving God,
> thank you for showing us in Jesus
> that you're always with us in any circumstances,
> offering both hope and challenge from within the situation.
> Thank you for showing us in Moses
> that that is how you have always liked to work.
> So, be within this service –
> call us, challenge us and fill us with your hope;
> forgive us for our pessimism and lack of trust,
> and help us live as your people in our day-to-day lives.
> Amen.

Based on Week 2

> Loving God,
> we are here because you have called us –
> your people,
> ready to move on wherever you choose to lead.
> Help us in our worship
> to be ready to leave behind those things
> that make our lives less than you want them to be,
> and to trust you for the hope and promise you have in store.
> Amen.

Based on Week 3

Loving God,
thank you for the freedom we enjoy
that enables us to be here,
to live openly as Christian people,
to journey with you in hope.
Thank you for all the things that give our lives
a healthy sense of structure –
that enable us to learn and to grow.
Please forgive us when we turn law into oppression,
or freedom into anarchy and selfishness,
and help us learn the love that is at the heart of your law.
Through Jesus Christ our Lord.
Amen.

Word and action – use whichever is appropriate

From Week 1

You can either give the cards out as people arrive, and then ask them to work in groups, or have a supply of cards at the front and a few children with pens to act as scribes, and do the exercise with the whole congregation. First, though, have the story read and point out how the hope of the Israelites was concealed among them even when they did not know it was there.

Now, ask the congregation to think of signs of hope. There's a lot of pessimism around these days, to do with declining congregations, lack of Christian presence in the media, and so on – but could it be that the very hope the church is seeking is concealed among you in the gifts and interests of its members? Perhaps you feel your fellowship can offer a renewed sense of community to an increasingly individualist world? Or, maybe, you have rooms that could be used for community activities and promote greater contact? Maybe you have retired people with skills that could be offered to others as a sign of God's love?

(You'd do well to have a few examples up your sleeve before you begin, from your own local knowledge.) If you feel that your particular church is so well blessed that you don't need to look for signs of hope, then you can still do the exercise, thinking of the church in the nation as a whole.

Write the ideas on the cards and put them among the 'bulrushes'. Then you can act surprised: we spend so much time praying and hoping for God to come to our rescue, and the hope's right here, concealed among us all the time. Perhaps we're all a bit like bulrushes, hiding God's hope from the world!

From Week 2

Before the service, get some children to help blow up the balloons and attach them to the chains.

After the story has been read, divide the congregation into groups and give each group a ball and chain. Ask them to think among themselves of the things that enslave people today, and write them on the links of their chain. They might like to think about local or national issues, or some of them may want to ask what holds the church back and prevents it from moving on. After a short time, let someone from each group come forward and share their ideas.

You can then say, if you like, that the next task will be to analyse the ideas on the chains and see where God might be calling the church into a liberating mission (probably beginning with itself). Why not suggest a Passover supper (it doesn't *have* to be on Maundy Thursday) and ask people to come in their outdoor clothes, walking boots if they have them, and with staffs in their hands – symbolically ready to move whenever God calls – and discuss the ideas over the meal?

From Week 3

Get the volunteer into the cell or behind the barred window (you may find it best for them to be in position before the service starts) and ask them why they're there. Why have they locked themselves away from the congregation? How much you hype this up will depend on your congregation and the acting ability of the 'prisoner' – the important thing to make clear is that the person doesn't feel safe outside the cell.

Now, get the congregation talking about how they can help people not to feel afraid – bearing in mind that many people outside the church find it very difficult to cross the threshold. What kinds of rules can you put in place to help people feel safe?

Examples might include not looking down on people who dress shabbily, not discriminating against people on racial grounds (or on the grounds of the football team they support!). It should go without saying, but not gossiping about people might be a good one.

This activity could be done either in groups or with the whole congregation together. Whichever you do, write up the rules they come up with. Then turn to the person in the cell and ask them if they feel safe to come out now (it may be best if it's pre-arranged that they will say 'yes' to this question!) Then, when they have rejoined the congregation, you can simply point out that rules aren't supposed to be a burden – we all need some kind of structure before we can enjoy our freedom! In the exercise you've just done, it was the lack of rules that caused the person to be locked up – good ground rules enabled them to be free! The purpose of God's law was to provide a safe place where people could enjoy freedom.

Now, have the story read in either narrative or dramatised form.

Song 2

Offering

This may be introduced as a token of the obedience we offer to God, not fearfully or reluctantly, but joyfully and freely, to enable his true freedom to be enjoyed by others.

Offertory prayer

> Loving God,
> you have made us to be free,
> and invited us freely to share in your creative work.
> So here, in trust and obedience to your call,
> we gladly offer you ourselves and our gifts,
> that the world may know your love.
> Amen.

Song 3

Reading

Matthew 22:35-40 read from a standard Bible. Introduce it with words such as: Jesus gives us in very few words a summary of the essence of God's law – the heart of the commandments given to Moses and all the mass of laws that flowed from them.

Talk (optional)

If you feel it appropriate (and if time permits) point out that Moses, the lawgiver, was also the person God chose to set the people free – no mere coincidence! So the ethical content of our faith is neither to be harshly imposed, damaging people's lives, nor lightly ignored as though it doesn't matter. Acting in truly loving ways is the heart of it.

Notices and family news

Prayers of intercession

These could be led entirely by the minister or other adult(s), and/or could include some prayers written by the children themselves – or simply some points that they have raised in discussion.

Song 4

Closing prayer/benediction

Unit 2
The Prophets – Elijah

Overview of the unit

Theme: There's more to being a prophet than meets the eye

We take three key events:

Week 1: The drought, and the widow of Zarephath

Elijah, a refugee from Queen Jezebel, finds asylum with a woman in need and they help each other.

Week 2: Mount Carmel

Elijah wins a contest with the prophets of the false god, Baal.

Week 3: Elijah at the cave

Once more a refugee, Elijah finds God in an unexpected way.

All-age worship

Here, you may choose to focus on any one of the three sub-themes, but place it in the context of the overall story and theme: there's more to being a prophet than meets the eye. So while the specific theme chosen will be emphasised in the choice of 'Word and action' material, some of the art and craft work the children have done in the other weeks will be used to decorate the church and set the context of the wider story.

Important note

✔ The ticked activities in Weeks 1-3 are intended as the link material for the 'Word and action' slot in the all-age worship. You will only need to do this in one of the three weeks – depending on which week's sub-theme is going to be the main emphasis in the service.

Week 1: The drought, and the widow of Zarephath

Thinking about it

What's the point?

Being a prophet is about a lot more than just foretelling the future. It begins with a really close relationship with God that allows someone to be a means whereby God can show his love to others.

Doing it

Prayer

Loving God,
thank you for calling all of us
to show your love in the world.
Help us to experience your love here,
as we share it with one another.
Amen.

From the known to the unknown

Can the children remember times when someone has helped them, and they've been able to help in return? Has that sort of encounter ever turned out to be the start of a new friendship – or perhaps just of getting to know someone a bit better than before? If you have some examples of your own that can ring bells with the children, that will be useful, too.

Tell the story: 1 Kings 17:8-24

(See page 44 for a dramatised version of this story.)

Prophet and loss

Can you imagine having just enough food for one last meal – and knowing that after that you're going to starve to death? I can't – most of us will probably never know what that feels like – but let me introduce you to two people who know exactly how it feels.

Imagine the scene. Close your eyes, and we're going back in time – back, back, to before anyone we know was born . . . back to the time when Jesus was born, but we're not stopping; back even further to – oh, there's King Solomon building the temple – we've gone too far. Forward a bit: that's it – about, oh, eight or nine hundred years before Jesus was born. We're a little way off from the place that happened, too – in Zarephath, which is actually outside Israel, to the north of Galilee. It's really hot – I mean, so hot that nothing will grow. And a widow called Anna and her son Joe are going to have that last meal I mentioned.

So, there's Anna, out gathering sticks for firewood when she sees this weird-looking guy. He's sitting on the ground to take the weight off his blistered feet, and his clothes look as though he's hiked across a desert in them – probably because he has. 'Excuse me, missus,' he says to her, 'but I could really murder a drink. Got a bit of water, have you?'

Now, remember, there's been no rain for yonks, so water's like gold – well, better, actually: what use is gold when you're thirsty? Still, Anna thinks, they're going to die anyway, so why not help this poor old man?

'Yes, OK – I'll go and get you some,' she says. Then, as she walks away, she can't believe her ears.

'A nice bit of bread,' the man calls out. 'That'd be really cool.'

Anna turns round. 'Bread?' she repeats, incredulously. 'Bread! Look, mister, I've got just enough flour left to mix with about three drops of olive oil that's left in the jar, and I'm going to make a last meal for Joe and me – Joe's my boy – and then we're going to die of starvation. Give you bread? I think not, somehow.'

'Right,' says the man, 'I'll tell you what. I'm a prophet, see – holy man – me and God, we're sort of close, you know. And he's promising that if you do this thing for me, your flour jar will never run out, and there'll always be olive oil in the bottle. So, how about it?'

Well, I ask you – here's this guy with his clothes in tatters and his feet growing fungus, who's obviously forgotten what water feels like on the skin, telling her he's God's agent and this is her big break. Would you believe him?

No, neither would I – but, for some reason, Anna *does* believe him – and the next thing she knows she's making this bread from the flour and oil and sitting down to eat it with her son, Joe, and – oh, did I tell you the prophet's name was Elijah? Well, that's put that right, now, hasn't it.

But, you know, it's amazing. From that moment on, every time Anna goes to look for flour, she finds some in the jar. And every time she uses that last drop of olive oil from the bottle, some more appears. 'This is unbelievable!' she says. 'You're obviously a good sort to have around.'

Well, things go on OK for a while, but then Joe gets ill. I mean, really ill – like I hope you've never been – probably the heat and the water shortage that did it, but no one really knows. Anyway, nothing they do can save him, and he dies. 'Oh, I get it!' Anna screams at Elijah. 'This is what comes of having a holy man under my roof – you've reminded God of something I did wrong and he's punishing me for it by killing my child.' Well, don't be too hard on her – there are still people around even today who think that God does that kind of thing.

Anyway, Elijah doesn't argue – just says, 'Give the boy to me,' and takes him and puts him on his own bed. Then he prays like he's never prayed before. 'Hey, God, what's the story? I mean, just what d'you think you're doing? This woman's been really kind to me, and you go and do a horrible thing like this to her?' Then he prays, 'O God, give the lad his life back!' Nothing happens, so he says it again. Still nothing. Three times, he has to say it – three! – and suddenly, Joe starts breathing again. So Elijah gets him off the bed and straight downstairs to his mother. 'Hey,' he says, 'have I got news for you – here he is!'

Well, if Anna thought the flour and the oil were impressive, she's got to be *seriously* impressed by this! 'No doubt about it,' she says. 'You're a man of God all right – I mean, why God should want to speak through someone with your dress sense, I don't really know – but he obviously does.'

Respond to the story

Discussion

How do the children think Anna felt when she had so little and this stranger was begging from her?

- sad that she couldn't help?
- embarrassed?
- angry that he was bothering her with his problems when she had so many of her own?

Two poor people helped each other. What do the children learn from that?

- that however little we've got, we can always find a bit of kindness for someone else?
- that it's not always the obvious people who have the answers?

Song

One or more of the following songs might be used here and/or in the all-age worship:

I walk by faith
Jehovah Jireh, God will provide
Take my hands, Lord
When I needed a neighbour

Art and craft

 On a flip-chart pad, or other large sheet of paper, draw the outline of a jar that could be used for storing flour. (See 'Word and action' in the all-age worship for how this would be used.) You'll need to enclose most of the sheet within the outline to give plenty of space to write inside the 'jar'. You might like to prepare the children for the all-age worship by giving them a chance to discuss the question the congregation will be asked there, so that they're ready to make their own contribution to that session.

Draw or paint a picture of Elijah asking Anna for help.

This is the key picture, but you might want to do others in addition to it, such as:

- the flour jar and oil bottle
- the 'family' sharing a meal

Drama

See the next page for a dramatised version of the story.

Drama: Prophet and loss

Narrator	Can you imagine having just enough food for one last meal — and knowing that after that you're going to starve to death? I can't — most of us will probably never know what that feels like — but let me introduce you to two people who know exactly how it feels. Imagine the scene. Close your eyes, and we're going back in time — back, back, to before anyone we know was born . . . back to the time when Jesus was born, but we're not stopping; back even further to — oh, there's King Solomon building the temple — we've gone too far. Forward a bit: that's it — about, oh, eight or nine hundred years before Jesus was born. We're a little way off from the place that happened, too — in Zarephath, which is actually outside Israel, to the north of Galilee. It's really hot — I mean, so hot that nothing will grow. And a widow called Anna and her son Joe are going to have that last meal I mentioned — oh, you can open your eyes now, by the way. So, there's Anna, out gathering sticks for firewood when she sees this weird-looking guy. He's sitting on the ground to take the weight off his blistered feet, and his clothes look as though he's hiked across a desert in them — probably because he has.
Elijah	Excuse me, missus, but I could really murder a drink. Got a bit of water, have you?
Narrator	Now, remember, there's been no rain for yonks, so water's like gold — well, better, actually: what use is gold when you're thirsty? Still, Anna thinks, they're going to die anyway, so why not help this poor old man?
Anna	Yes, OK — I'll go and get you some.
Narrator	Then as she walks away, she can't believe her ears.
Elijah	A nice bit of bread. That'd be really cool.
Anna	Bread? Bread! Look, mister, I've got just enough flour left to mix with about three drops of olive oil that's left in the bottle, and I'm going to make a last meal for Joe and me — Joe's my boy — and then we're going to die of starvation. Give you bread? I think not, somehow.
Elijah	Right, I'll tell you what. I'm a prophet, see — my name's Elijah — anyway, me and God, we're sort of close, you know. And he's promising that if you do this thing for me, your flour jar will never run out, and there'll always be olive oil in the bottle until the end of the water shortage. So, how about it?
Narrator	Well, I ask you — here's this guy with his clothes in tatters and his feet growing fungus, who's obviously forgotten what water feels like on the skin, telling her he's God's agent and this is her big break. Would you believe him? No, neither would I — but, for some reason, Anna *does* believe him — and the next thing she knows she's making this bread from the flour and oil and sitting down to eat it with her son, Joe, and Elijah. But, you

know, it's amazing. From that moment on, every time Anna goes to look for flour, she finds some in the jar. And every time she uses that last drop of olive oil from the bottle, some more appears.

Anna

This is unbelievable! You're obviously a good sort to have around.

Narrator

Well, things go on OK for a while, but then Joe gets ill. I mean, really ill – like I hope you've never been – probably the heat and the water shortage that did it, but no one really knows. Anyway, nothing they do can save him, and he dies. Anna really yells at Elijah.

Anna

Oh, I get it! This is what comes of having a holy man under my roof – you've reminded God of something I did wrong and he's punishing me for it by killing my child.

Narrator

Well, don't be too hard on her – there are still people around even today who think that God does that kind of thing.

Elijah

Give the boy to me.

Narrator

Elijah takes Joe and puts him on his own bed. Then he prays like he's never prayed before.

Elijah

Hey, God, what's the story? I mean, just what d'you think you're doing? This woman's been really kind to me, and you go and do a horrible thing like this to her? O God, give the lad his life back!

Narrator

Nothing happens, so he says it again. Still nothing. Three times, he has to say it – three! – and suddenly, Joe starts breathing again. So Elijah gets him off the bed and straight downstairs to his mother.

Elijah

Hey, have I got news for you – here he is!

Narrator

Well, if Anna thought the flour and the oil were impressive, she's got to be *seriously* impressed by this!

Anna

No doubt about it, you're a man of God all right – I mean, why God should want to speak through someone with your dress sense, I don't really know – but he obviously does.

45

Colour this picture, using crayon, paint or felt-tips

God doesn't always use the obvious people.
Colour the pictures which look most like the people God chose in this story.

WORDSEARCH

Find the following words in the grid: ELIJAH,
WIDOW, ZAREPHATH, PROPHET, FLOUR, OIL,
WATER, ILLNESS, DEATH, LIFE, MIRACLE

```
E L C A R I M L L I F T
R S S E N L L I E L I J
P R O F E T W O D I W F
R E L I L Z A R E P A L
O W I D O O W A T R T O
P M I R A C U L E H E U
H E W I D O S R A B R R
E L A G H E L J A T E R
T I T D T L I F L I F E
D J E H A L M I R A C L
C Z A R E P H A T H H J
I L L N D S S D E A T R
```

Colour the dotted shapes to find the
food God has provided for the widow

Week 2: Elijah at Mount Carmel

Thinking about it

What's the point?

A difficult one, actually! We need to be careful not to equate the cult of Baal simplistically with the great world religions that are now part of our multi-cultural scene. Attitudes of Christians towards other religions vary widely, of course, but none of us wants to encourage futile 'My God's better than your God' jibes in the playground. However, this story's part of our Scriptures and children need to learn it. A more creative approach would be to think in terms of the worship of things that don't satisfy us: fashions, fads, momentary pleasures – not least the pursuit of material 'success' to the exclusion of more satisfying friendships and interests.

Doing it

Prayer

Loving God,
thank you for bringing us here together.
Thank you for all the really important things that you give to us,
like friendship, love, and all that can make us truly happy.
Help us to value your love,
and to show it to one another.
Amen.

From the known to the unknown

Have the children ever really wanted something – and thought that if they had that, they'd finally be really happy? How long has it been before they've thought the same thing about something else? Have some of them, perhaps, got forgotten toys that were once idolised but quickly lost their appeal? It might be helpful to share your own childhood (or more recent!) experiences of that to encourage them not to be embarrassed – after all, it's something that we're all prone to at some times in our lives. In this story, Elijah shows that only God can truly satisfy us.

Tell the story: 1 Kings 18:17-39

(See page 50 for a dramatised version of this story.)

Elijah's big firework

Now, the trouble with running away is that at some point you generally have to come back.

So, there are King Ahab and Queen Jezebel, thinking Elijah's gone for good, when who should turn up but – yes, you've guessed it – Elijah. 'Oh, good grief!' Ahab says. 'Here's trouble.'

Elijah thinks that's a bit rich. 'It's not me that's the troublemaker,' he says. 'You're the one who's been unfaithful to God – running off and worshipping Baal instead of God. Well, it's showdown time: get all the prophets of Baal to Mount Carmel and we'll see which God is real.'

Now, it may seem strange, but for some reason, Ahab does what Elijah says – probably thinks it's the quickest route to a quiet life. Anyway, before long, they're all there at Mount Carmel: 450 prophets of the false god, and Elijah for the real one. And they've got a good audience, too – Elijah's seen to that. 'Right,' he says, 'it's "make your mind up" time, folks. Whom do you really believe in – God or Baal?' No answer. 'Fair enough,' says Elijah, 'let's have a couple of animal sacrifices. All you lot who follow Baal, kill your bull and put it on the altar, and I'll do one for the true God. And the God who sends down fire from heaven and sets his sacrifice burning – well, that's who we worship. OK?'

'Fair enough!' they all say. So, the prophets of Baal start it off. They put the bull on the altar, and they start praying. That's in the morning. By lunch time they're still there, still praying, dancing and shouting enough to wake the dead – and the meat on the altar's as raw as when they put it there. No fire, no answer from Baal, not a very good morning's work at all, really.

Elijah – well, he's just loving it. 'Shout louder!' he jeers at them. 'I mean, he *is* a god, isn't he? Well, he's probably having a bit of a think – you know how absent-minded that can make you. Or maybe he's just wandered off some-where. There again, he may have gone on a long journey. Mind you, I could be wrong – he's probably just dozing – shout louder and wake him up.'

Well, the prophets of Baal are getting themselves into a right old frenzy – but all the shouting in the world isn't getting them very far, and they've hardly got the strength to prance around any more. Come the evening, the sacrifice is still there – not a flicker of fire to be seen.

'My turn,' Elijah says. 'Now, let's begin by rebuilding this altar to the true God – the altar you tried to get rid of.' So he gathers the stones, rebuilds the altar, and then does a very odd thing – he digs a trench all round God's altar. Then he puts the meat for the sacrifice on the altar with some wood for burning – just as Baal's prophets did earlier. Then he really gets carried away. It's as if he thinks the challenge is too easy: he sends for water – buckets and buckets of the stuff – and he pours it all over the meat on the altar. The meat's absolutely soaked, the altar's running wet, and the trench he dug is full of muddy water. And he thinks it's going to burn!

By now the people are getting a bit tired – they've been there all day, watching Baal's prophets making fools of themselves – but something keeps them there to see whether Elijah's God can do better.

Elijah starts to pray. 'Lord God – the God of all our history – let's see your power now. Show us all that you're the only God around here – well, any-where, actually – and that I'm truly your servant, OK? I mean, I've done all this because you told me to – so let's make sure everyone understands that. Come on, God – answer my prayer – show them all that you're God and you want them to turn back to you.'

Have you ever seen anything more unlikely? There's this meat on the altar, water all over it, great puddles of the stuff in all the hollows, the altar absolutely dripping, and Elijah wants it to burn! Well, I've got news for you. It does. Before anyone has time to blink, the whole altar seems to be ablaze. I mean, we've all seen fire, but this is serious stuff. It burns up all the meat, all the sopping wet wood underneath it, and it's not finished yet.

It's so hot even the stones themselves burn – and the water in the trench around the altar's got no chance. Everything's gone. Now, is that fire, or is that fire!

Now, you'd really think that nobody would mess with Elijah after that, wouldn't you – but no, before long Elijah's back on the run again because Queen Jezebel's out to get him. Which only goes to show that winning arguments isn't what it's about – it's people's hearts that need changing, not just their minds.

Respond to the story

Discussion

What might the people have thought when Elijah poured all that water over the altar?

- that he'd gone crazy?
- that even God stood no chance of making *that* burn?

Why do the children think that Queen Jezebel was so angry afterwards?

- because she didn't like being defeated?
- because she already hated Elijah and this just made things worse?
- because she didn't want to worship the true God?
- anything else?

Song

One or more of the following songs might be used here and/or in the all-age worship:

God is good, God is great
God is good, we sing and shout it
Praise God in his holy place
This little light of mine

Art and craft

 Make a 'robot' out of scrap materials. (See 'Word and action' in the all-age worship for how this would be used.) The finished article should be recognisably human in appearance. Make sure it can stand up on its own – if you can put it on a pedestal, that's all the better.

Draw or paint a picture of the altar on fire – perhaps with Elijah standing beside it.

This is the key picture, but you might want to do others in addition to it, such as:

- Elijah running away from an angry Queen Jezebel

Drama

See the next page for a dramatised version of the story.

Drama: Elijah's big firework

Narrator	Now, the trouble with running away is that at some point you generally have to come back. So, there are King Ahab and Queen Jezebel, thinking Elijah's gone for good, when who should turn up but – yes, you've guessed it – Elijah. Ahab isn't pleased.
Ahab	Oh, good grief! Here's trouble.
Elijah	It's not me that's the troublemaker. You're the one who's been running off and worshipping Baal instead of God. Well, it's showdown time: get all the prophets of Baal to Mount Carmel.
Narrator	Now, for some strange reason, Ahab does what Elijah says – probably thinks it's the quickest route to a quiet life. Anyway, before long, they're all there at Mount Carmel: 450 prophets of the false god, and Elijah for the real one. And they've got a good audience, too – Elijah's seen to that.
Elijah	Right, it's 'make your mind up' time, folks. Whom do you really believe in – God or Baal?
Bystander	Um – well, I'm not sure, really. It depends what you mean by 'God'.
Elijah	Right. Let's have a couple of animal sacrifices. All you lot who follow Baal, kill your bull and put it on the altar, and I'll do one for the true God. And the God who sends down fire from heaven and sets his sacrifice burning – well, that's who we worship. OK?
Bystander	Fair enough!
Narrator	So, the prophets of Baal start it off. They put the bull on the altar, and they start praying.
Baal's prophets	Send the fire, Baal! Send the fire!
Narrator	That's in the morning. By lunch time they're still there, still praying, dancing and shouting enough to wake the dead – and the meat on the altar's as raw as when they put it there. No fire, no answer from Baal, not a very good morning's work at all, really.
Elijah	[*Taunting*] Shout louder! I mean, he *is* a god, isn't he? Well, he's probably having a bit of a think – you know how absent-minded that can make you. Or maybe he's just wandered off somewhere or gone on a long journey. There again, he's probably just dozing – shout louder and wake him up.
Baal's prophets	Send the fire, Baal! Send the fire!
Ahab	Jezebel won't like this, Elijah. She won't like it at all.
Narrator	Well, come the evening, the prophets of Baal are getting themselves into a right old frenzy – but all the shouting

in the world isn't getting them very far, and they've hardly got the strength to prance around any more. The sacrifice is still there – not a flicker of fire to be seen.

Bystander   I'm tired of this game. Can we play another one?

Elijah   My turn. Now let's begin by rebuilding this broken altar to the true God – the altar you tried to get rid of.

Ahab   Jezebel *really* won't like this. You're in for it now, Elijah.

Narrator   He gathers the stones, rebuilds the altar, and then does a very odd thing – he digs a trench all round God's altar. He puts the meat for the sacrifice on the altar with some wood for burning – just as Baal's prophets did earlier. Then he sends for water – buckets and buckets of the stuff – and he pours it all over the meat on the altar. The meat's absolutely soaked, the altar's running wet, and the trench he dug is full of muddy water.

Bystander   And he thinks it's going to burn!

Narrator   By now the people are getting a bit tired – they've been there all day, watching Baal's prophets making fools of themselves – but something keeps them there to see whether Elijah's God can do better. Elijah starts to pray.

Elijah   Lord God – the God of all our history – let's see your power now. Show us all that you're the only God around here – well, anywhere, actually – and that I'm truly your servant, OK? I mean, I've done all this because you told me to – so let's make sure everyone understands that. Come on, God – answer my prayer – show them all that you're God and you want them to turn back to you.

Narrator   Have you ever seen anything more unlikely?

Bystander   I haven't.

Narrator   There's this meat on the altar, water all over it, the altar absolutely dripping, and Elijah wants it to burn! Well, I've got news for you. It does. Before anyone has time to blink, the whole altar seems to be ablaze. I mean, we've all seen fire, but this is serious stuff. It burns up all the meat, all the sopping wet wood underneath it, and it's not finished yet. It's so hot even the stones themselves burn – and the water in the trench around the altar's got no chance. Everything's gone. Now, is that fire, or is that fire!

Bystander   It's amazing

Ahab   It's most inconvenient. Jezebel really won't like it at all.

Narrator   Now, you'd really think that nobody would mess with Elijah after that, wouldn't you – but no, before long Elijah's back on the run again because Queen Jezebel's out to get him. Which only goes to show that winning arguments isn't what it's about – it's people's hearts that need changing, not just their minds.

Colour this picture, using crayon, paint or felt-tips

Enjoy GOOD things worship only GOD

WORDSEARCH

Find the following words in the grid:
MONEY, SUCCESS, FASHION,
CHOICE, FAME, FITNESS, SPEED,
WORK, INFORMATION,
TECHNOLOGY, SHOPPING

```
I N F O R M A T I O N B
T G D R N O I H S A F C
E F A E M O N E U S A H
C F A S E O N E C U S O
H O R M G P J D C C H I
N A M E E T S P E C I C
O K N O W S E D S E O E
L M O N E T X K S S R H
O D I N F O R M R H S A
G I T N E S Y E N O M M
R I S H O P P I N G W E
F P Y G O L O N H C E T
```

Get the computer off the altar and into the office!

52

Week 3: Elijah at the cave

Thinking about it

What's the point?

God doesn't always work in the spectacular ways we might expect – so it's easy to think nothing's happening and to lose hope. Elijah found that things aren't always as they seem.

Doing it

Prayer

Loving God, thank you for this time we have together.
Please help us to learn about you through each other.
Amen.

From the known to the unknown

Get the children to think about the different kinds of friends they have. Some are brash, confident, impressive. We all need people like that, sometimes. But do they know people who are quiet, thoughtful, who are easy not to notice? Have they ever been surprised by how helpful those people can be?

Sometimes, God works in ways we don't expect.

Tell the story: 1 Kings 19:1-21

(See page 56 for a dramatised version of this story.)

Elijah listens and learns

Some people never give up! I mean, Elijah's just pulled off a pretty impressive stunt and shown up the false god Baal for the impostor he is, and you'd think Queen Jezebel would just back off gracefully. But no – instead, she's after Elijah's blood again. So, not for the first time, Elijah heads for the hills – runs as if his life depends upon it (which, of course, it does). To cut a slightly longer story short, he ends up at a cave in the mountains. 'No one will find me here,' he thinks. 'I'll get a bit of peace here.'

Wrong, Elijah! There's one person who'll find you, wherever you are – and what's going to happen to you now is hardly peaceful! So, who's the person who can find you wherever you are – apart from the truant officer, that is? Well, it's God, isn't it. So Elijah's just thinking he's got the place to himself when he hears this voice. 'Hey, Elijah, what are you doing here?'

Elijah can hardly believe God's asking him such a silly question. 'What am I doing here?' he says. 'Look, I've done all right by you, haven't I? I mean, I've really tried – but what have the people of Israel done? Broken all their promises, that's what – not to mention smashing up all your worship places. Oh, yes, and they've killed all your prophets, too – I'm the only friend you've got left in the world, and now they're after me. I think the reason I'm hiding here might be just a touch obvious, don't you?'

Now, I guess God might have been a bit sad about that – I mean, there have always been people who thought they were the only friend God had, but he probably expected Elijah to know better. 'Go and stand at the cave entrance,' he tells Elijah, 'and whatever happens, you stay there, OK – because I'm going to be passing that way and you just might learn something.'

So, Elijah goes to stand just inside the mouth of the cave. He's hardly got there when there's this huge hurricane. I mean, huge enough to break rocks into little bits – have *you* ever seen wind do that? Great big rocks are flying past the cave entrance and breaking into little fragments. Naturally, Elijah thinks God must be in the wind – but not a word does he hear. Nothing at all.

Next, it's an earthquake – everything's shaking like a jelly at a children's party, and Elijah thinks God must be in the earthquake. But he's not. Then comes a fire – seems as if the whole world's going up in smoke: great clouds of soot and ash falling around the mouth of the cave, but no sign of God anywhere.

Well, Elijah's just about had enough by now. He doesn't know what God's trying to pull, but he'd have had less trouble if he'd stayed where Queen Jezebel could find him. 'Well,' he thinks, 'if God passed by I must have missed him! And he turns to go back. But what do you think happens next?

Next, he hears nothing at all. Just silence – a really eerie silence – the kind where you just know that something's waiting to happen. So Elijah wraps his cloak round his head, creeps to the front of the cave entrance and peers out. It's so quiet, not even the leaves on the trees are rustling, and Elijah's sure something big's about to happen – that God's going to show himself now, and it's going to be even more spectacular than everything that's just happened all put together. Very gingerly, he steps out of the cave on to the mountainside. Then it happens. God's voice is really quiet, so he can hardly hear it, but he knows jolly well who it is. 'Elijah,' God whispers, 'what are you doing here?'

Well, that sets Elijah off again. 'I've been really good,' he says, 'really enthusiastic – you know? I've done everything you asked me to, but they've been and gone and ignored you – there's not an altar or a prophet standing upright in the whole country – except me. I'm the only friend you've got left, and they're after me, too. Hey, haven't we been through this before?'

'Go home, Elijah,' God says to him. 'On the way, you'll meet a few other friends of mine, like Hazael and Jehu – they're going to be kings – and a guy called Elisha who's going to be a prophet. He doesn't know it yet, but he will. Now, it's going to turn nasty – I won't lie to you about that – but there'll be another seven thousand friends of mine left to pick up the pieces, so you're hardly the last one, are you?'

So off goes Elijah, finds this Elisha chap and sets him on as his own servant – well, young prophets have to start at the bottom, you know. He's got a lot to learn, but he'll have a good teacher. Elijah's a much wiser man now.

Respond to the story

Discussion

What do the children think God was trying to teach Elijah?

- That God doesn't always work the way we expect?
- That quiet speaking can be more powerful than a lot of noise?

How do they think Elijah felt when he found there were seven thousand other friends of God when he'd thought he was the only one?

- Pleased?
- Encouraged?
- Perhaps rather silly?
- (The older children may pick up on the possibility of Elijah's actually being disappointed, or at least his arrogance deflated, to find out that he wasn't as unique as he'd thought!)

Song

One or more of the following songs might be used here and/or in the all-age worship:

Be still and know that I am God
Be still, for the presence of the Lord
Calm me, Lord
Silent, surrendered

Art and craft

✔ Let the children make some untuned percussion instruments, using whatever they can. (See 'Word and action' in the all-age worship for how this would be used.) Raid the church kitchen if it helps, for wooden spoons, tins and pans, as well as making (for example) maracas from plastic cups with rice in them. Get them also to make a simple megaphone out of paper or card, and choose a child with a clear but not loud voice to speak through it. Explain to them how all this will be used on the day, and then let them have a bit of fun practising!

Draw or paint a picture of Elijah at the mouth of the cave.

This is the key picture, but you might want to do others in addition to it, such as:

- an earthquake or a landslide
- a great fire
- trees bending in the wind

Drama

See the next page for a dramatised version of the story.

Drama: Elijah listens and learns

Narrator	Some people never give up! I mean, Elijah's just pulled off a pretty impressive stunt and shown up the false god Baal for the impostor he is, and you'd think Queen Jezebel would just back off gracefully. But no – instead, she's after Elijah's blood again. So, not for the first time, Elijah heads for the hills – runs as if his life depends upon it (which, of course, it does). To cut a slightly longer story short, he ends up at a cave in the mountains.
Elijah	No one will find me here. I'll get a bit of peace here.
Narrator	Wrong, Elijah! There's one person who'll find you, wherever you are – and what's going to happen to you now is hardly peaceful! So, who's the person who can find you wherever you are – apart from the truant officer, that is? Well, it's God, isn't it. So Elijah's just thinking he's got the place to himself when he hears God's voice.
God	Hey, Elijah, what are you doing here?
Elijah	What am I doing here? Look, I've done all right by you, haven't I? I mean, I've really tried – but what have the people of Israel done? Broken all their promises, that's what – not to mention smashing up all your worship places. Oh, yes, and they've killed all your prophets, too – I'm the only friend you've got left in the world, and now they're after me. I think the reason I'm hiding here might be just a touch obvious, don't you?
Narrator	Now, I guess God might have been a bit sad about that – I mean, there have always been people who thought they were the only friend God had, but he probably expected Elijah to know better.
God	Go and stand at the cave entrance, and whatever happens, you stay there, OK – because I'm going to be passing that way and you just might learn something.
Narrator	So, Elijah goes to stand just inside the mouth of the cave. He's hardly got there when there's this huge hurricane. I mean, huge enough to break rocks into little bits – have *you* ever seen wind do that? Great big rocks are flying past the cave entrance and breaking into little fragments.
Elijah	A wind like this – God must be in it.
Narrator	But not a word does Elijah hear. Nothing at all. Next, it's an earth-quake – everything's shaking like a jelly at a children's party.
Elijah	Surely, God's got to be in this!
Narrator	But he's not. Then comes a fire – seems as if the whole world's going up in smoke: great clouds of soot and ash falling around the mouth of the cave, but no sign of God anywhere. Well, Elijah's just about had enough by now. He doesn't know what God's trying to pull, but he'd have had less trouble if he'd stayed where Queen Jezebel could find him.
Elijah	Well, if God passed by I must have missed him!

Narrator	But what do you think happens next? Next, he hears nothing at all. Just silence – a really eerie silence – the kind where you just know that something's waiting to happen. So Elijah wraps his cloak round his head, creeps to the front of the cave entrance and peers out. It's so quiet, not even the leaves on the trees are rustling, and Elijah's sure something big's about to happen.
Elijah	God's going to show himself now, and it's going to be even more spectacular than everything that's just happened all put together.
Narrator	Very gingerly, he steps out of the cave on to the mountainside. Then it happens. God's voice is really quiet, so he can hardly hear it, but he knows jolly well who it is.
God	Elijah, what are you doing here?
Elijah	I've been really good, really enthusiastic – you know? I've done everything you asked me to, but they've been and gone and ignored you. There's not an altar or a prophet standing upright in the whole country – except me. I'm the only friend you've got left, and they're after me, too. Hey, haven't we been through this before?
God	Go home, Elijah. On the way, you'll meet a few other friends of mine, like Hazael and Jehu – they're going to be kings – and a guy called Elisha who's going to be a prophet. He doesn't know it yet, but he will. Now, it's going to turn nasty – I won't lie to you about that – but there'll be another seven thousand friends of mine left to pick up the pieces, so you're hardly the last one, are you?
Narrator	So off goes Elijah, finds this Elisha chap and sets him on as his own servant – well, young prophets have to start at the bottom, you know. He's got a lot to learn, but he'll have a good teacher. Elijah's a much wiser man now.

Elijah thinks he's the only friend God has left, but he isn't. Can you find 9 more, hiding in the picture?

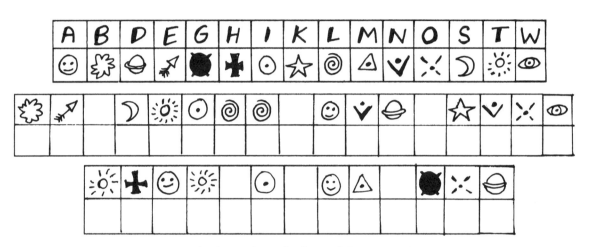

Crack the code to find a well-known saying

WORDSEARCH

Find the following words in the grid:
ELIJAH, PROPHET, CAVE, JEZEBEL, HURRICANE, EARTHQUAKE, FIRE, SILENCE, STILLNESS, HAZAEL, JEHU, ELISHA

58

Week 4: All-age worship

Opening song

A song praising and celebrating the faithfulness of God

Welcome and statement of the theme

Get one or more of the children to point out or hold up the pictures as you sum up the story:

In Junior Church during the past few weeks, we've been learning about Elijah, who represents the prophets. We heard the story of Elijah and the widow – how they helped one another when God brought them together. Then we heard about Elijah and the prophets of the false god Baal, and how Elijah won the contest but not the hearts and minds of the people – especially Queen Jezebel who swore she'd make him pay for it. Then we read about Elijah at the cave – the one he was hiding in when he ran away from Queen Jezebel – and how he learnt that God doesn't always work by the spectacular methods we sometimes expect. That's the general picture, but today we're going to concentrate on: [*Name the episode of your choice*]

Prayer – use whichever is appropriate

Based on Week 1

Loving God, thank you for your prophets
who show your love to us.
Thank you for putting us in a world with other people –
for giving us one another to help and to be helped.
Please forgive us when we fail to notice what others have to offer,
or what we should be offering to them,
and help us to be like prophets ourselves
in showing your love to the world.
Amen.

Based on Week 2

Loving God, thank you for being who you are –
a God who loves, who cares, who feels the things we feel.
Please forgive us when we forget you
and go after other things that may seem easier to see and touch,
but in the end don't satisfy us.
Help us to be faithful to you, as you are to us.
Amen.

Based on Week 3

Loving God, we meet here to worship you.
Help us to remember that listening is part of worship,
and to recognise you at the moments
when we might least expect to hear you.
Please forgive us for the times when we don't recognise you

because you don't fit our prejudices,
and help us to be open to you in whatever way you speak to us.
Amen.

Word and action – use whichever is appropriate

From Week 1

Have the story read, in either narrative or dramatised form, and then point out the picture on the flip-chart. Just as God brought Elijah and the widow together to support each other, so he's done with this congregation. So you're now going to fill the flour jar with the great gifts God has given you in each other. These could include practical skills in cooking, carpentry or drain-clearing, artistic talents that can raise people's spirits or enliven worship, wonderful memories that the older people can use to entertain the younger – no doubt many things special to your church that writers of worship books would never think of.

As they're thought of, write them up, starting at the bottom, and see if you can fill the flour jar. Here is God's provision for his people, given to them in one another!

From Week 2

Point out the 'robot' and say that the children made it all themselves. Clever, aren't they? Get a child to stand alongside it, and ask the congregation to name the advantages of the 'robot' – for example: it doesn't answer back; it doesn't need getting up in the morning; it doesn't make a fuss in the supermarket . . .

So, would people like to have it in place of the real thing (a beautiful example of which is of course standing just beside it)? So, what's the advantage of a child? Again, you can have some fun – it certainly doesn't always do what you want it to. At the end of the day, though, it's real and it can give you something the best of robots will never give you.

And if you need me to spell that one out, then we've really got a problem! Now have the story read in either narrative or dramatised form, and simply comment that it's not entirely difficult to understand the people of Israel looking for a god who didn't make the same kind of demands that a real one would – the trouble was that it was ultimately unsatisfying, just like a robot would be in place of a child. You can now ask for any other examples of 'false gods' that look good but don't ultimately satisfy. Most of us have got plenty of them in our homes, and that's OK just as long as they stay in their place!

From Week 3

Tell the congregation that some of the children have a message for them, and because it's God's message they're going to make sure it really grabs their attention. Let the children with instruments make as much noise as they can, while the child with the megaphone repeats through it, 'Be still and know that I am God.'

After a few moments (you won't want very long!) stop the racket and ask the congregation if they can hear. Repeat a couple of times if you think it's appropriate, and then get the child to say the verse without the megaphone and without the accompaniment.

Now have the story read, in either narrative or dramatised form, and then let the congregation sing *Be still and know* – quietly, while still seated.

Song 2

Offering

This may be introduced as symbolic of our willingness to offer ourselves as prophetic signs of God's love in the world.

Offertory prayer

Holy God,
accept the gifts we bring,
both of our possessions and of ourselves,
and so perfect them
that we may be visible signs of your love in the world.
Amen.

Song 3

Reading

1 Corinthians 13 read from a standard Bible. Introduce it with words such as: St Paul places prophecy, along with all God's gifts, in the vital context of his love, which is at the heart of everything.

Talk (optional)

If you feel it appropriate (and if time permits) you can point out that the prophets weren't just about foretelling the future. That was only part of their role. They were reminders to the people of what it meant to be loved by God, and the responsibilities that involves for us in living as loved and loving people. For Elijah that meant both practical caring, as with the widow of Zarephath, and denunciation of all that was unloving – which was how he came to be always upsetting Queen Jezebel!

Notices and family news

Prayers of intercession

These could be led entirely by the minister or other adult(s), and/or could include some prayers written by the children themselves – or simply some points that they have raised in discussion.

Song 4

Closing prayer/benediction

Unit 3
Jesus: perfecting the law and the prophets in love

Overview of the unit

Theme: Jesus fulfils the law and the prophets

We take three key events:

Week 1: Transfiguration

Jesus is seen in the company of Moses and Elijah.

Week 2: The parable of the Samaritan (Jesus fulfils the law in love)

Jesus refuses to put a limit on love.

Week 3: Nazareth sermon (Jesus fulfils the prophets in justice)

Jesus sets out the heart of his mission in the Nazareth sermon.

All-age worship

Here, you may choose to focus on any one of the three sub-themes, but place it in the context of the overall story and theme: Jesus fulfils the law and the prophets. So while the specific theme chosen will be emphasised in the choice of 'Word and action' material, some of the art and craft work the children have done in the other weeks will be used to decorate the church and set the context of the wider story.

Important note

✔ The ticked activities in Weeks 1-3 are intended as the link material for the 'Word and action' slot in the all-age worship. You will only need to do this in one of the three weeks – depending on which week's sub-theme is going to be the main emphasis in the service.

Week 1: Transfiguration

Thinking about it

What's the point?

Being seen by his disciples in the company of Moses and Elijah should have made the point that he wasn't throwing out all their traditions but bringing them to fulfilment. The law and the prophets were ways God had shown his love for his people – and Jesus was going to raise that revelation to new heights.

Doing it

Prayer

Loving God,
thank you for giving us each other,
and this place to be together.
Help us to build up our friendship
and learn more about you in the things we do today.
Amen.

From the known to the unknown

Do the children have any 'rules' at home? They may be very simple ones like 'No breakfast before you're dressed' or 'Brush your teeth after you've eaten' – and they almost certainly won't be written down – but all homes have some sort of rules even if they're not often stated explicitly. We can't live entirely by those rules, though – we need people to love us, to guide us, to help us learn about life and love – and for most of us our parents and siblings do that.

In the same way, God gave his people rules – remember Moses and the ten commandments? – and he also gave them special people – the prophets – to help them learn his ways. Finally, he brought it all together in Jesus, and that's what we're going to look at today.

Tell the story: Mark 9:2-10

(See page 68 for a dramatised version of this story.)

Moses, Elijah and Jesus

There are some pretty strange stories in the Bible – and this is one of them. So, I want you to imagine we're back in the time when Jesus was living his earthly life. Now, see if you can work out where we are. The air's a bit on the cool side for the time of day; we're all a bit out of breath; and there's this incredible view – we can see for miles. So, where do you think we are?

OK, so we're up a mountain. Jesus has come up here with his closest friends, Peter, James and John. And he hasn't told them why. Perhaps we can hear them talking.

'I don't know what this is all about,' Peter's saying, 'but it'd better be good. I'm a seaman, I am – not a mountain man.'

James and John probably have their own theories. We know James and John were a bit full of themselves – wanted to be the top people, and thought Jesus was going to give them power. We can just hear John saying, 'He's brought us up here to look at our kingdom, that's what. One day, we'll be in charge of all this – isn't that right, James?'

'You – in charge?' Peter scoffs. 'Jesus wouldn't put you two in charge of a compost heap – he's got more sense!'

Just a minute, though – what's happening? Jesus is starting to look really odd – his robe is starting to glow. And as we watch, it gets brighter and brighter, until it's shining so brightly it's dazzling to look at!

'All right,' we can hear James saying, 'if you're so all-fired clever, explain that.'

No one can, of course – but it's about to get even more weird. Suddenly there are two other men there, talking with Jesus. Not ordinary men – to be honest, they look a bit wild. They've got long beards, untidy hair, and clothes that most people certainly wouldn't wear to church, let alone to meet Jesus face to face – well, not without giving them a good ironing, anyway.

'It's Moses and Elijah!' James whispers.

'Of course it is,' says John. 'Anybody can see that.'

Now why it's so obvious isn't really – um – obvious, but they all seem agreed about it. The people talking with Jesus are Moses and Elijah. Now, Peter's always been one to get carried away – so you can imagine how he reacts. 'Hey, Teacher!' he says. 'Is this terrific, or is this terrific! Why don't we make three shelters here – one for you, one for Moses and one for Elijah? Then we could just stay here, all the time, couldn't we?'

The truth is, poor old Peter's really as scared as everyone else and doesn't honestly know what to say – so instead of saying nothing he's saying anything – anything that comes into his head, without thinking about it first. Peter's trouble is he's got a mouth like a tumble-dryer – he just opens it and whatever happens to be at the front falls out!

Anyway, back to the story. There they are, all pretty frightened and trying not to show it, when the whole scene gets even more spooky. I mean, on a clear day, when you can see for miles, suddenly there's this thick, black cloud. No rain – just a cloud, coming from nowhere, and it covers everybody. And then there's a voice – seems to come from the cloud itself. 'This is my Son,' it booms. 'This is the special one – pay attention to him.'

So, we've got Jesus, with his robes shining and glittering like disco lighting; we've got these two old guys – Moses and Elijah, who we all know have been dead for centuries; we've got a big, dark cloud; and we've got a voice coming from nowhere. What d'you make of all that, then?

Too late! It's gone! There's Peter with his face buried in the grass, pretending to be looking for grasshoppers but shaking and trembling as if it's going out of fashion, and James and John gazing around them with their mouths open – and Jesus, standing there all alone as though nothing's happened at all.

'Time to go,' he says. 'We can't stay up here all the time – there's work to do.'

So, they start off down the mountain again, with James and John all agog to find out what it meant.

'Come on, Jesus – what was all that about?' James is asking him.

'That's not for you to know at the moment,' Jesus says, mysteriously. 'And don't go blabbing about this to everyone else, either – got it? You can tell them all about it after I've risen from the dead.'

'Risen from the dead?' says Peter. 'Now, there's an idea – but what does it mean?'

And so they walk away, down the mountain again – gassing away among themselves, and leaving us to work out what it was all about.

Respond to the story

Discussion

How do the children think Peter and his friends felt, seeing these strange things happen all around them?

- awestruck?
- fearful?
- mystified?

A question perhaps for the older children. Can they remember what Moses and Elijah each represent? (Moses the law and Elijah the prophets.) Why do they think they were together with Jesus on the mountain?

- to show that Christ is really at the centre of all our religious traditions?
- to show that Jesus valued the traditions and wasn't just out to destroy them?

Song

One or more of the following songs might be used here and/or in the all-age worship:

Jesus is the lighthouse
Jesus' love is very wonderful
Lord, the light of your love is shining
Majesty

Art and craft

✔ On a flip-chart pad, either draw a figure of Christ or, if you prefer, a cross to represent his presence. (See 'Word and action' in the all-age worship for how this would be used.) Explain to the children that you're going to help the congregation to see how Jesus holds together all the things that are important to us in our faith. You might also want to prepare some cards – about postcard size – that can be Blu-Tacked around the picture during the service. Alternatively, you might prefer simply to write things up with a marker pen.

Draw or paint a picture of Jesus with Moses and Elijah.

This is the key picture, but you might want to do others in addition to it, such as:

- Jesus and his friends climbing up the mountain

Drama

See the next page for a dramatised version of the story.

Drama: Moses, Elijah and Jesus

Narrator	Now, there are some pretty strange stories in the Bible – and this is one of them. So, I want you to imagine we're back in the time when Jesus was living his earthly life. Now, see if you can work out where we are. The air's a bit on the cool side for the time of day; we're all a bit out of breath; and there's this incredible view – we can see for miles. So, where do you think we are?
	OK, so we're up a mountain. Jesus has come up here with his closest friends, Peter, James and John. And he hasn't told them why. Perhaps we can hear Peter talking.
Peter	I don't know what this is all about, but it'd better be good. I'm a seaman, I am – not a mountain man.
Narrator	James and John probably have their own theories. We know James and John were a bit full of themselves – wanted to be the top people, and thought Jesus was going to give them power. We can just hear what John might say.
John	He's brought us up here to look at our kingdom, that's what. One day, we'll be in charge of all this.
Peter	You two – in charge? Jesus wouldn't put you two in charge of a compost heap – he's got more sense!
Narrator	Just a minute, though – what's happening? Jesus is starting to look really odd – his robe is starting to glow. And as we watch, it gets brighter and brighter, until it's shining so brightly it's dazzling to look at!
James	All right, if you're so all-fired clever, explain that.
Narrator	No one can, of course – but it's about to get even more weird. Suddenly there are two other men there, talking with Jesus. Not ordinary men – to be honest, they look a bit wild; They've got long beards, untidy hair, and clothes that most people certainly wouldn't wear to church, let alone to meet Jesus face to face – well, not without giving them a good ironing, anyway.
James	It's Moses and Elijah!
John	Of course it is – anybody can see that.
Narrator	Now why it's so obvious isn't really – um – obvious, but they all seem agreed about it. The people talking with Jesus are Moses and Elijah. Now, Peter's always been one to get carried away – so you can imagine how he reacts.
Peter	Hey, Teacher! Is this terrific, or is this terrific! Why don't we make three shelters here – one for you, one for Moses and one for Elijah? Then we could just stay here, all the time, couldn't we?
Narrator	The truth is, poor old Peter's really as scared as everyone else and doesn't honestly know what to say – so instead of saying nothing he's saying anything – anything that comes into his head, without thinking about it first. Peter's trouble is he's got a mouth like a tumble-dryer – he just opens it and whatever happens to

	be at the front falls out! Anyway, back to the story. There they are, all pretty frightened and trying not to show it, when the whole scene gets even more spooky. I mean, on a clear day, when you can see for miles, suddenly there's this thick, black cloud. No rain – just a cloud, coming from nowhere, and it covers everybody. And then there's a voice – seems to come from the cloud itself.
God	This is my Son. This is the special one – pay attention to him.
Narrator	So, we've got Jesus, with his robes shining and glittering like disco lighting; we've got these two old guys – Moses and Elijah, who we all know have been dead for centuries; we've got a big, dark cloud; and we've got a voice coming from nowhere. What d'you make of all that, then?
	Too late! It's gone! There's Peter with his face buried in the grass, pretending to be looking for grasshoppers but shaking and trembling as if it's going out of fashion, and James and John gazing around them with their mouths open – and Jesus, standing there all alone as though nothing's happened at all.
James	Time to go. We can't stay up here all the time – there's work to do.
Narrator	So, they start off down the mountain again, with James and John all agog to find out what it meant.
James	Come on, Jesus – what was all that about?
Jesus	That's not for you to know at the moment. And don't go blabbing about this to everyone else, either – got it? You can tell them all about it after I've risen from the dead.
Peter	Risen from the dead? Now, there's an idea – but what does that mean?
Narrator	And so they walk away, down the mountain again – gassing away among themselves, and leaving us to work out what it was all about.

Colour this picture, using crayon, paint or felt-tips

Can you spot 6 differences between the pictures?

WORDSEARCH

Find the following words in the grid:
MOSES, ELIJAH, JESUS, TRANSFIGURED, MOUNTAIN, CLOUD, SHINING, SON, PETER, JAMES, JOHN

```
T R A N S F I G U R J D
S H I N N I A T N U O M
V U N Y M O S H I N H O
P E S E R O H J O A N S
C L O E N A S C L O U E
L I J A J A M E S J O H
O S H I N I N E S O D R
U E L I J A M O U H T E
D E R U G I F S N A R T
J A M I S E S O U D R E
M O S H I N I N G C H P
M O U N T A I D P E T E
```

Week 2: The parable of the Samaritan
(Jesus fulfils the law in love)

Thinking about it

What's the point?

Jesus approved of the summary of the law as love towards God and neighbour – and then identified the neighbour in horrifyingly comprehensive terms. The people we're most afraid of, whom we tend to keep at arm's length, God calls our neighbours.

Doing it

Prayer

Loving God,
we're here together to worship you
and to learn about you.
Help us to learn about each other, as well,
and to understand one another better. Amen.

From the known to the unknown

Have the children ever been surprised by kindness from someone they didn't like? Have they been helped by someone they thought might ignore or hurt them? Perhaps they've thought someone very unfriendly only to find out that that person had thought the same thing of them!

Tell the story: Luke 10:25-37

(See page 74 for a dramatised version of this story.)

God's basic law of love

Have you noticed how some people get a real hang-up about rules? Now, don't get me wrong: we all need rules to help us live properly – it's just that some folk think they're the answer to absolutely everything. And that's how Jesus came to tell this story – well, one very like it, anyway. A man asked him, 'What do I have to do to get to heaven?'

Well, Jesus knew what the guy was up to – he was trying to catch Jesus out. So Jesus just said, 'What does the law say? What d'you read in your Bible?'

'Easy!' the man answered. 'Love God – like, really love him – and love your neighbour the way you love yourself.'

'Fine,' said Jesus. 'Do that and you'll not go wrong.'

Well, the man wasn't satisfied with that, was he! 'Yeah, yeah, yeah,' he said, 'but what do you mean by neighbour?' Well, he asked for it! Jesus answered by telling a story, a lot like this one:

Imagine someone walking from Jerusalem to Jericho. Jesus didn't tell us his name, but we'll call him Bart. So, Bart decides he wants to go to Jericho. He ought to know better, because the Jericho road's really dangerous – not because of the traffic, but because of bandits. The hills around are crawling with them, and they'll rob anything that moves! Still, Bart's not worried by that – he thinks he can take care of himself. So, off he goes – and it's not long before he's lying at the side of the road, covered in blood, and thinking he's going to die.

Then he hears footsteps. 'Thank you, God!' he says. 'Someone's going to help me.' Very painfully, he turns his head to look down the road, and sees a priest coming along.

The priest doesn't even come near to him – just crosses right over to the other side of the road and keeps going. 'Sorry,' he calls out, 'can't touch blood at the moment – I've got a service to take, and worshipping with blood on my hands would be against all the rules. Sorry, and all that.' And to Bart's utter amazement, he scuttles past and leaves him there.

Next guy along is a Levite – another kind of religious leader – and Bart really thinks he's going to help, but exactly the same thing happens. 'I'm ever so sorry,' the Levite calls as he passes, 'but you might be dead for all I know – and if I touch a dead body it'll take me weeks to get clean again. Sorry, but it's the rules.' And off he goes, on the other side of the road.

Well – what's poor old Bart to do? He can't move because of the blood-loss and sunstroke, and he really thinks he's going to die. So, when he hears more footsteps coming, he doesn't really hope for very much at all – especially when he sees that it's a Samaritan. Now, what you need to know is that Samaritans and Jews don't talk to each other. In fact, they hate one another. Jews think Samaritans have got their religion all wrong, and Samaritans think Jews are stuck-up snobs – and that *they've* got their religion wrong, too!

'Well, this is no good,' Bart thinks, 'no good at all. Here I am, lying here with blood leaking out everywhere and the people I thought would help me didn't – I've got no chance with a lousy, rotten Samaritan.' But then an incredible thing happens. The Samaritan – let's call him Joe – goes over to where Bart's lying, and looks down at him.

'Good grief!' Joe exclaims. 'You've really been in the wars, haven't you! I'll soon get you somewhere safe.' Then he kneels down on the road and gives Bart first aid – cleans up his wounds, bandages them – and then says, 'Let's get you on to my donkey – there's an inn just down the road where you can be looked after.'

So, next thing Bart knows is that he's in a nice clean bed in a fancy hotel, being looked after by the innkeeper, and Joe – the 'lousy, rotten Samaritan' – is handing over his own money to pay the bill! 'Just make sure he's looked after,' Joe says, 'and next time I'm here I'll pay you whatever else I owe.'

So, that's the story Jesus told. Then he turned to the man who'd asked the question, and said, 'So, who do *you* think was a neighbour to the injured man?'

'That's easy!' the man answered. 'The one who helped him.'

'Great!' Jesus answered. 'So why don't you just stop trying to catch me out and go and do the same?'

That wasn't what the man had wanted to hear. He'd always thought keeping the rules was simple – but he'd reckoned without God's basic rule of love, and he'd never imagined it would mean he had to be nice to Samaritans!

Respond to the story

Discussion

How do the children think the man felt when the priest and Levite didn't help him?

- angry?
- desperate?
- mystified?

How might he have felt when he realised that the Samaritan was actually being kind to him?

- amazed?
- 'Where's the catch'?
- excited by what he had learnt?

What *had* he learnt?

Song

One or more of the following songs might be used here and/or in the all-age worship:

Brother, sister, let me serve you
God made a boomerang and called it love
Take my hands, Lord
When I needed a neighbour

Art and craft

✔ On a large board or sheet of paper (at least flip-chart size) draw a picture of a castle, leaving enough room around the outside to write things up. (See 'Word and action' in the all-age worship for how this would be used.) Explain to the children that a castle would be somewhere where we would feel safe, and in the all-age worship we're going to think about the people we would shut out because they threaten us – just as the Jews and Samaritans shut each other out because of fear.

Draw or paint a picture of the victim lying at the roadside.

This is the key picture, but you might want to do others in addition to it, such as:

- the priest scurrying away
- the Samaritan stopping to help

Drama

See the next page for a dramatised version of the story.

Drama: God's basic law of love

Narrator	Have you noticed how some people get a real hang-up about rules? Now, don't get me wrong: we all need rules to help us live properly – it's just that some folk think they're the answer to absolutely everything. And that's how Jesus came to tell this story – well, one very like it, anyway. A lawyer asked him a question.
Lawyer	What do I have to do to get to heaven?
Narrator	Well, Jesus knew what the guy was up to – he was trying to catch Jesus out.
Jesus	What does the law say? What d'you read in your Bible?
Lawyer	Easy! Love God – like, really love him – and love your neighbour the way you love yourself.
Jesus	Fine. Do that and you'll not go wrong.
Lawyer	Yeah, yeah, yeah, but what do you mean by neighbour?
Narrator	Well, he asked for it! Jesus answered by telling a story, a lot like this one:
Jesus	Imagine someone walking from Jerusalem to Jericho.
Narrator	Jesus didn't tell us his name, but we'll call him Bart.
Jesus	So, Bart decides he wants to go to Jericho. He really ought to know better, because the Jericho road's really dangerous – not because of the traffic, but because of bandits. The hills around are crawling with them, and they'll rob anything that moves! Still, Bart's not worried by that – he thinks he can take care of himself. So, off he goes – and it's not long before he's lying at the side of the road, covered in blood, and thinking he's going to die. Then he hears footsteps.
Bart	Thank you, God! Someone's going to help me.
Jesus	Very painfully, he turns his head to look down the road, and sees a priest coming along. The priest doesn't even come near to him – just crosses right over to the other side of the road and keeps going.
Priest	[*Calls*] Sorry, can't touch blood at the moment – I've got a service to take, and worshipping with blood on my hands would be against all the rules. Sorry, and all that.
Jesus	And to Bart's utter amazement, he scuttles past and leaves him there. Next guy along is a Levite – another kind of religious leader – and Bart really thinks he's going to help, but exactly the same thing happens.
Levite	I'm ever so sorry, but you might be dead for all I know – and if I touch a dead body it'll take me weeks to get clean again. Sorry, but it's the rules.
Jesus	And off he goes, on the other side of the road. Well – what's poor old Bart to do? He can't move because of the blood-loss and sunstroke, and he really thinks he's going to die. So, when

he hears more footsteps coming, he doesn't really hope for very much at all – especially when he sees that it's a Samaritan. Now, what you need to know is that Samaritans and Jews don't talk to each other. In fact, they hate one another. Jews think Samaritans have got their religion all wrong, and Samaritans think Jews are stuck-up snobs – and that *they've* got their religion wrong, too!

Bart   Well, this is no good, no good at all. Here I am, lying here with blood leaking out everywhere and the people I thought would help me didn't – I've got no chance with a lousy, rotten Samaritan.

Jesus   But then an incredible thing happens. The Samaritan – let's call him Joe – he goes over to where Bart's lying, and looks down at him.

Joe   Good grief! You've really been in the wars, haven't you! I'll soon get you somewhere safe.

Jesus   Then Joe kneels down on the road and gives Bart first aid.

Joe   Let's get you on to my donkey – there's an inn just down the road where you can get looked after.

Jesus   So, next thing Bart knows is that he's in a nice clean bed in a fancy hotel, being looked after by the innkeeper, and Joe – the 'lousy, rotten Samaritan' – is handing over his own money to pay the bill!

Joe   Just make sure he's looked after, and next time I'm here I'll pay you whatever else I owe.

Narrator   So, that's the story Jesus told. Then he turned to the man who'd asked the question.

Jesus   So, who do *you* think was a neighbour to the injured man?

Lawyer   That's easy! The one who helped him.

Jesus   Great! So why don't you just stop trying to catch me out and go and do the same?

Narrator   That wasn't what the man had wanted to hear. He'd always thought keeping the rules was simple – but he'd reckoned without God's basic rule of love, and he'd never imagined it would mean he had to be nice to Samaritans!

The Samaritan's taking a big risk by stopping to help. Can you see 6 robbers hiding in the picture?

Finish the sentences and you will find the essence
of God's law by reading down the starburst column

This Story is about the real meaning of God's

The Samaritan Put the injured man on his

One of those who Passed by was a

Jesus says the person I like least is still my

WORDSEARCH
Find the following words in the grid: LAW, LOVE, GOD, NEIGHBOUR, JERUSALEM, JERICHO, SAMARITAN, BANDITS, PRIEST, LEVITE, DONKEY, INN

```
L E V D O N K E Y E S T
P R S A M A R I T A A N
N A A T I R A M A S H M
A B N E I G H B O U R E
T L A T O D O N K E S L
I B E C H A N D I T S A
R L O V C V S A M A R S
A D O N I E Y S B M G U
M B S V R T L A W R O R
A P R I E S E K N O D E
S A M A J I T A N D E J
L O V P R I E S T N N I
```

Show the Samaritan the way
to get the injured man to the inn

76

Week 3: Jesus preaches at Nazareth (Jesus fulfils the prophets in justice)

Thinking about it

What's the point?

We say Jesus is the fulfilment of the prophecies – but that doesn't just mean that he made them come true. Jesus brought the prophets to their fulfilment by embodying the love of God which they, in their different ways, had called people to recognise. Whether that was in challenging authority, warning of the consequences of injustice or offering practical care to people, that love was their driving force, and Jesus embodied and became the ultimate revelation of it.

Doing it

Prayer

Thank you, God,
for showing your love to us,
in your stories, in your prophets,
and most of all in Jesus.
Help us in our time together to find your love in one another.
Amen.

From the known to the unknown

Have the children ever had the experience of thinking someone was coming to help them, and then finding themselves getting a ticking off instead? Perhaps they'd got lost and their parents' relief came out as anger? I remember tilting my chair back during a meal and nearly falling into the fire. My father saved me by grabbing the chair, and I was somewhat surprised to find that, far from being pleased I was safe – or proud of having saved me – he was angry with me for being so stupid, especially when he'd repeatedly warned me of the danger and been ignored! Maybe you have your own examples you can share. Make a joke of it, but let the children see there's a serious point. People thought Jesus was going to be 'Mr Nice Guy', but they found he had a challenging edge to him as well.

Tell the story: Luke 4:16-30

(See page 80 for a dramatised version of this story.)

Jesus challenges us with love

Can you imagine a full-scale riot breaking out during a service because of something the preacher said? Well, Jesus started one at his synagogue in Nazareth.

Imagine the scene. The place is full of people – nearly everybody in the town goes to worship – and one of them is Jesus. He's just come back from taking some time out to listen to God, so they're probably pleased to see him – and then someone asks him to read the Bible reading.

'It's from the book of Isaiah,' Jesus announces. 'This is what the prophet Isaiah says: "God's chosen me, and given me his Spirit – he's put his power into me. I've to go and tell his good news. Not just any old good news – good news specially for all the poor people. Oh, yes – I'm here to set all captives free. I'm here to make blind people see again, and everyone who's being bullied by people in power – well, they're going to be free of that. This is it, folks – this is the time of God's choosing when he's going to change things in this here world."'

Now, everyone's paying attention. They've all completely forgotten the gossip they'd been going to share – and no one's even bothering to look for who's wearing the nicest clothes. Suddenly, they've got the idea that this morning might be interesting. So they're all just waiting there, as quiet as Accrington Stanley stadium on a Saturday. And every single eye is looking straight at Jesus. 'Right now,' he says, 'this prophecy has come true – right here where you are!'

Just in front of you, you can see old Rachel, the flower steward, lean across to her husband. 'Ooh,' she says, 'don't he talk lovely! Don't you think so, Ben?'

Ben doesn't look so happy, though. 'Who's he think he is?' he grumbles. 'His dad's the local carpenter – what does he know about prophecy?'

Jesus hasn't finished yet, though. 'I know what you're all thinking!' he says. 'You're wondering why I don't do miracles here, like the ones you've heard I've done elsewhere.'

'Well?' Ben calls out. 'Why don't you?'

'I'll tell you,' Jesus answers. 'Because prophets can't work in their home towns – people won't accept them.'

'What d'you know about it?' Ben objects. 'You're just a local boy!'

Jesus is really getting going now. His eyes are shining, and his face is full of colour as he looks straight at Ben. 'Look in your Bible,' he says, 'and ask yourself: why did Elijah have to go and help a foreign widow – weren't there enough widows in Israel? And what about Naaman – weren't there people in Israel who needed healing at that time – so why did Elisha only heal a foreigner?'

Old Rachel turns to her husband again. 'He's got a point, ain't he?' she says. 'Prophets always get driven away, don't they.'

'Load of rubbish!' Ben objects. 'If he goes on talking like that he's going to get thrown out of here.'

Mind you, you can hardly hear what they're saying because the whole congregation's shouting insults at Jesus and telling him to go away – but I won't tell you what they're actually saying, because they aren't as polite as I am.

Then, suddenly, everyone's on their feet all around us. The noise is amazing – everyone's shouting, and stamping their feet, and it feels like Spurs have lost at home and we're in the wrong enclosure. Even old Rachel has got caught up in it. 'Get him!' she's shouting. 'Throw him out! Go on, parson – give him a bunch of fives.'

Suddenly, Ben's at it, too. 'Take him to the cliff!' he's shouting. 'Throw him off the edge!' Well, I won't tell you all the details – it's not very nice seeing religious people behave like that – but, right at the last minute, Jesus sort of fixes the mob with his eyes, and he seems to pull them up short. You can almost hear them thinking, 'What are we doing? How did we get from worshipping God to trying to kill the preacher?'

Jesus begins to walk forward, and as he does so the crowd fall back and let him through. But it just goes to show – it's not just other people who need prophets to remind them to love each other; religious people like us need it, too.

Respond to the story

Discussion

Why do the children think the people got so angry with Jesus?

- because he reminded them they weren't as good as they thought?
- because they'd gone to worship wanting to feel good, not be challenged?

Song

One or more of the following songs might be used here and/or in the all-age worship:

Change my heart, O God
Let love be real
Let's get fit
Lord, look into my heart
This little light of mine

Art and craft

✔ On a flip-chart pad or whiteboard, draw a picture of a happy, smiling face looking out from a window, and cut out from card or paper some strips to form prison bars (but don't stick them on yet). (See 'Word and action' in the all-age worship for how this would be used.) An alternative would be to make a screen with a window in it, for a child to stand behind and look through. This might be more effective in the service, but will obviously require more resources. Explain to the children that you're going to be thinking in the service about Jesus' promise to set people free.

Draw or paint a picture of Jesus reading from the scroll.

This is the key picture, but you might want to do others in addition to it, such as:

- the congregation getting angry
- the crowd on the cliff edge

Drama

See the next page for a dramatised version of the story.

Drama: Jesus challenges us with love

Narrator

Can you imagine a full-scale riot breaking out during a service because of something the preacher said? Well, Jesus started one at his synagogue in Nazareth. Imagine the scene. The place is full of people – nearly everybody in the town goes to worship – and one of them is Jesus. He's just come back from taking some time out to listen to God, so they're probably pleased to see him – and then someone asks him to read the Bible reading.

Jesus

I'll read from the book of Isaiah. This is what the prophet Isaiah says: 'God's chosen me, and given me his Spirit – he's put his power into me. I've to go and tell his good news. Not just any old good news – good news specially for all the poor people. Oh, yes – I'm here to set all captives free. I'm here to make blind people see again, and everyone who's being bullied by people in power – well, they're going to be free of that. This is it, folks – this is the time of God's choosing when he's going to change things in this here world.'

Narrator

Now, everyone's paying attention. They've all completely forgotten the gossip they'd been going to share – and no one's even bothering to look for who's wearing the nicest clothes. Suddenly, they've got the idea that this morning might be interesting. So they're all just waiting there, as quiet as Accrington Stanley stadium on a Saturday. And every single eye is looking straight at Jesus.

Jesus

Right now, this prophecy has come true – right here where you are!

Narrator

Just in front of you, you can see Rachel, the flower steward, lean across to her husband.

Rachel

Ooh, don't he talk lovely! Don't you think so, Ben?

Ben

Who's he think he is? His dad's the local carpenter – what does he know about prophecy?

Jesus

I know what you're all thinking! You're wondering why I don't do miracles here, like the ones you've heard I've done elsewhere.

Ben

Well? Why don't you?

Jesus

I'll tell you. Because prophets can't work in their home towns – people won't accept them.

Ben

What d'you know about it? You're just a local boy!

Narrator

Jesus is really getting going, now. His eyes are shining, and his face is full of colour as he looks straight at Ben.

Jesus

Look in your Bible, and ask yourself: why did Elijah have to go and help a foreign widow – weren't there enough widows in Israel? And what about Naaman – weren't there people in Israel who needed healing at that time – so why did Elisha only heal a foreigner?

Rachel

He's got a point, ain't he? Prophets always get driven away, don't they.

Ben

Load of rubbish! If he goes on talking like that he's going to get thrown out of here.

Narrator	Mind you, you can hardly hear what they're saying because the whole congregation's shouting insults at Jesus and telling him to go away – but I won't tell you exactly what they're saying, because they aren't as polite as I am. Then, suddenly, everyone's on their feet all around us. The noise is amazing – everyone's shouting, and stamping their feet, and it feels like Spurs have lost at home and we're in the wrong enclosure. Even Rachel has got caught up in it.
Rachel	Get him! Throw him out! Go on, parson – give him a bunch of fives.
Ben	Take him to the cliff! Throw him over the edge!
Narrator	Well, I won't tell you all the details – it's not very nice seeing religious people behave like that – but, right at the last minute, Jesus sort of fixes the mob with his eyes, and he seems to pull them up short. You can almost hear what they're thinking.
Rachel	What are we doing?
Ben	How did we get from worshipping God to trying to kill the preacher?
Narrator	Jesus begins to walk forward, and as he does so the crowd fall back and let him through.
Rachel	It just goes to show, don't it!
Ben	Yes, it's not just the people out there who need prophets to remind them to love each other; it's us, too.

Colour this picture, using crayon, paint or felt-tips

What are the right ways to respond if someone's saying things we disagree with?

Listen?

Refuse to listen?

Shout them down?

Politely say what we think?

WORDSEARCH

Find the following words in the grid:
JESUS, NAZARETH, SYNAGOGUE, ISAIAH, PROPHET, CAPTIVES, FREE, BLIND, SEE, CHANGE, WORLD

```
P R O P H I S A I A H N
B S Y N A G O C A P T I
L C H A N W O R L S U S
I S P R O P H E T Y E I
N A Z R J E S U W O R E
D X L E C H A G E D S E
H D S Y N A G O G C H R
Y U W O R L W G A H M F
S Y N H T E R A Z A N R
N A Z A R E T N C N V E
P R O P H E V Y N G H S
C A P T I V E S D E D E
```

Think about what they're saying?

Keep it friendly?

Week 4: All-age worship

Opening song

A song praising and celebrating the faithfulness of God

Welcome and statement of the theme

Get one or more of the children to point out or hold up the pictures as you sum up the story:

In Junior Church during the past few weeks, we've been learning about how both the law and the prophets – two principal strands of Jewish biblical tradition – were fulfilled by Jesus. We read the story of the Transfiguration in which Jesus was seen by his disciples conversing with Moses and Elijah – the traditional representatives of the law and the prophets. Then we looked at the parable of the Samaritan. Here, a lawyer rightly said that the law really boiled down to love for God and for neighbour, but asked, 'Who is my neighbour?' Jesus blew the whole concept wide open with the parable he told. And then we looked at Jesus' first sermon – at the synagogue in Nazareth – where he focused in on the prophetic concern with justice and got a dusty response from his congregation.

That's the general picture, but today we're going to concentrate on: [*Name the episode of your choice*]

Prayer – use whichever is appropriate

Based on Week 1

Loving God,
we thank you for all that has brought us here together –
all the journeys of faith that we've made,
the traditions we've come from,
the ideas and beliefs that have become important to us.
Most of all, though, we thank you
for meeting us in your Son Jesus Christ,
and drawing us together into a living community.
Please forgive us when we lose sight
of the living Christ within our ideas and traditions,
and help us to rediscover the joy of being in his presence.
Amen.

Based on Week 2

Thank you, loving God, for this time of worship.
Thank you that it is something we do together,
with people who are important to us.
Please forgive us for the times when we forget
about other people who aren't so obviously our friends,
and forget that you love them too.
Help us to be open to your people,
and to recognise them as our neighbours and your children.
Amen.

Based on Week 3

Holy God, we have come to worship you,
seeking warmth, consolation, good fellowship,
and many more things besides.
Help us also to be open to you
as you challenge us, question our assumptions,
and show your love by calling us to grow and to learn.
Please forgive us for the times
when we become complacent in our faith,
and open us all up to the exciting – and sometimes daunting –
challenge of your presence.
Amen.

Word and action – use whichever is appropriate

From Week 1

Ask the congregation to spend a few minutes in groups identifying the different Christian traditions that are vital to their faith. For some people, perhaps, it might be the centrality of scripture or of prayer; some might say believers' baptism (others, equally, might say infant baptism); the priesthood of all believers will possibly be an important concept to some while the freedom of the Holy Spirit in worship might be vital to others. Some people may say it's the simpler things like hospitality that are important to them; others may feel that theological concepts about the nature of the Eucharist have defining value. If you're using the cards, give each group a few and ask them to write the ideas down.

Call them to order and ask for some examples from the different groups. Someone might like to come forward and Blu-Tack the cards around the picture, or you could just ask them to call out while you write things up.

You should finish up with quite a list of what people regard as important aspects of the faith, all clustered around Jesus or the cross. You can then simply point out that it is Christ who is truly central to our faith, and he draws together a whole variety of principles and ideas. This is shown in the Gospels in the story of the Transfiguration, in which the two main elements of Jewish scripture – the law and the prophets – are brought together in the presence of Christ and become focused on him.

Now have the story read, in either narrative or dramatised form.

From Week 2

Have the story read, either in narrative or dramatised form, and point out that Jews and Samaritans feared each other, but Jesus said that God's law of love meant trying to see the people we fear as human beings.

So, here's a picture of what our homes and churches might represent to us: our castle – our safe place. Who are the groups of people we shut out of our safe place because we fear them? Think local, if you can. Do people feel intimidated by groups of young people in the streets at night? Is fear of crime a real problem in your area, or are people perhaps apprehensive because of drug or alcohol misuse?

Write these things up, and then ask how we can learn to understand better. Would it be good to invite a youth worker, probation officer, or perhaps a local police officer or mental health worker to come and speak?

Don't try and find a quick answer in the service, but be happy at least to have raised awareness and then refer the question to the appropriate church body for further thought.

Loving our neighbour – which Jesus has extended to mean everybody we're most afraid of – has to begin with an attempt to reach out and understand (which is not necessarily to approve), so that at least some of the barriers can begin to be lowered.

From Week 3

Have the story read in either narrative or dramatised form. Point out the picture, or get a child to stand behind the screen looking through the window. Remind the congregation that Jesus promised to set people free. So here's this person looking through the window at us – but is s/he free to come inside?

Get the congregation into groups (or if you prefer, just work with them as one group) to discuss what 'bars' there may be that prevent people coming. What is disabled access like? Can wheelchairs get to the Communion rail? Do you have a loop system for people who are hard of hearing? If you have a number of deaf people, has anyone thought about getting the services signed? What about blind people – what barriers are put in their way?

Another – related – issue might be about the dependency of the church on books for its worship. Not only blind people find books difficult; for people whose reading habits scarcely encompass the tabloid newspapers, being handed two or three sizeable books at the church door may be a real psychological barrier.

As obstacles are identified, write them on the bars and Blu-Tack them over the window in front of the face. (If you're using a real child, the smile can gradually be replaced by a frown!)

If you really do end up with no bars, then your church has really something to celebrate. If, as most will, you end up with more bars than you expected, you've identified some urgent agenda items for the councils of the church. You could even take the visual aid into a meeting, commended by the congregation for urgent attention.

Song 2

Offering

This may be introduced as symbolising our willingness, however imperfect, to offer ourselves fully to God, open to all that an experience of his love may hold.

Offertory prayer

Loving God, we offer you ourselves,
our lives, the things we hold dear,

for you to refine and use
so that the world may know your love.
Amen.

Song 3

Reading

Matthew 5:13-20 read from a standard Bible. Introduce it with words such as: Jesus emphasises that he has come not to abolish the great traditions, but to fulfil them.

Talk (optional)

If you feel it appropriate (and if time permits) you can reinforce the point that Jesus' whole life revealed the love which is at the heart of God's law, and which also drove the prophets to challenge injustice and corruption. This is not a love that smiles sweetly and avoids conflict; it's a love that cares so much that it hurts – and that cares enough to challenge all that is not for our well-being.

Notices and family news

Prayers of intercession

These could be led entirely by the minister or other adult(s), and/or could include some prayers written by the children themselves – or simply some points that they have raised in discussion.

Song 4

Closing prayer/benediction